EGYPT

LOST CIVILIZATIONS

The books in this series explore the rise and fall of the great civilizations and peoples of the ancient world. Each book considers not only their history but their art, culture and lasting legacy and asks why they remain important and relevant in our world today.

Already published:

The Barbarians Peter Bogucki
Egypt Christina Riggs
The Indus Andrew Robinson
The Persians Geoffrey Parker and Brenda Parker

EGYPT
LOST CIVILIZATIONS

CHRISTINA RIGGS

REAKTION BOOKS

In memory of my beloved Behemoth:

Under the lotus plants he lies,
  in the shelter of the reeds and in the marsh.
For his shade the lotus plants cover him;
  the willows of the brook surround him. (*Job 40:21–2*)

Published by Reaktion Books Ltd
Unit 32, Waterside
44–48 Wharf Road
London N1 7UX, UK

www.reaktionbooks.co.uk

First published 2017
Copyright © Christina Riggs 2017

Printed and bound in China

A catalogue record for this book is available from the British Library

ISBN 978 1 78023 726 8

CONTENTS

CHRONOLOGY

c. 4500–3000 BC	Predynastic era
c. 3000–2600 BC	Early Dynastic Period, Dynasties 1–3 Step Pyramid of Saqqara
c. 2600–2180 BC	Old Kingdom, Dynasties 4–6 Pyramids of Giza; Tomb of Ti
c. 2180–2050 BC	First Intermediate Period
c. 2050–1650 BC	Middle Kingdom, Dynasties 11–13
c. 1650–1550 BC	Second Intermediate Period
c. 1550–1070 BC	New Kingdom, Dynasties 18–20 A list of kings in the temple of Seti 1 at Abydos stretches back to the earliest days of Egyptian history; craftsmen working on tombs in the Valley of the Kings live – and die – in the village of Deir el-Medina
c. 1070–712 BC	Third Intermediate Period, Dynasties 21–24 The Greenfield Papyrus of Nestanebtasheru

712–332 BC	Late Period, Dynasties 25–30 and Persian occupation
332–30 BC	Ptolemaic Period, ending with reign of Cleopatra VII – contemporary with the Republican era in Roman Italy, when the Palestrina mosaic was created
30 BC–AD 395	Roman Period, when Egypt was part of the Roman Empire; Sigmund Freud's baboon, Herculaneum wall painting
395–640s	Byzantine Period, when Egypt was part of the Byzantine Empire, governed from Byzantium (modern-day Istanbul); Horapollo writes his guide to hieroglyphs
640s–969	Umayyad, Abassid and Tulunid Caliphates include Egypt
969–1171	Fatimid dynasty rules Egypt
1171–1250	Ayyubid dynasty, founded by Salah ad-Din (Saladin) rules Egypt
c. 1300	A *Mappa Mundi* made in England represents Egypt with the Old Testament granaries of Joseph
1250–1517	Mamluk rulers govern Egypt
1517	Conquest of Egypt by Ottoman sultan, Selim I

15th century	Renaissance Italy sees a rediscovery of ancient Greek and Latin texts, including several that discuss Egypt or originated there; Pavement of Siena Cathedral
16th century	Egyptian obelisk imported during Roman times is re-erected as part of Bernini's Four Rivers fountain in Rome
18th century	Freemasonry becomes popular among well-educated or aristocratic men in Europe and the new nation of America, which puts the Freemasonic symbol of an eye and a pyramid on the reverse of its Great Seal
1798–1801	Napoleon's invasion of Egypt, ending in defeat – and turning over to the British the Rosetta Stone and other antiquities; Vivant Denon leads a groups of French scientists, engineers and artists seeking to map and record both modern and ancient Egypt
1805	Muhamed Ali becomes *wali* (governor) of Egypt, under Ottoman rule, and encourages European-style industrialization to help cement his own power
1809	Publication of the first volume of the *Description de l'Égypte*; during a vogue for Egyptian-style design in Europe
1822	Jean-François Champollion announces his decipherment of hieroglyphs, based in part on the Rosetta Stone

1849	Death of Muhamed Ali, who is succeeded by his son and grandsons
1849–51	Maxime du Camp undertakes a photographic mission to Egypt on behalf of the French ministry of education
1851	The Crystal Palace (Great) Exhibition in Hyde Park, London, includes an Egyptian Court designed by Owen Jones, based on the colourful temples and statues he had seen in Egypt
1858	Said *pasha*, son of Mohamed Ali, appoints the French scholar Auguste Mariette to oversee the conservation of antiquities and monuments in Egypt
1860s onwards	Increasing European and American investment in the Egyptian cotton and sugar cane industries and corresponding increase in travel and tourism. From the 1870s, steamboats in use for the first 'package tours' to Egypt; Victorian scientists develop schemes of racial classification which are exploited by some to justify colonization and slavery; novels, paintings and popular culture depict a fantasy of 'ancient Egypt', with moonlit Nile views and barely clad Cleopatras
1867	The Ottoman sultan recognizes the title *khedive* (viceroy) for the rulers of Egypt, beginning with Said's successor Ismail

1869	Opening of the Suez Canal, funded by French shareholders, and celebrated with the premiere of Verdi's opera *Aida*
1875	British government purchases khedive Ismail *pasha*'s shares in the Suez Canal, after a financial crisis
1882	British military occupation of Egypt, to suppress a revolt led by Egyptian general Urabi *pasha*; establishment of the Egypt Exploration Society, a charity for British-sponsored excavations in Egypt. For the next forty years, the British government controls Egypt, and archaeological excavations extend throughout the country, with thousands of antiquities shipped to museums and collectors around the world
1902	The Museum of Egyptian Antiquities moves from Giza Palace to its current, Italian-designed building in central Cairo
1914	Britain proclaims Egypt a Sultanate, to oppose the Ottoman Empire during the First World War
1919	Egyptian Revolution, led by Sa'ad Zaghloul, presses Britain for Egyptian self-rule

1920s–30s	The Harlem Renaissance looks to ancient Egypt to represent African accomplishments in art and culture
1922	Britain declares Egypt independent but maintains control of foreign affairs; sultan Ahmed Fuad becomes King Fuad I. Discovery of the tomb of Tutankhamun leads to a stand-off between excavator Howard Carter and the Egyptian antiquities service over the ownership of the finds – all of which remain in Egypt
1928	Mahmoud Mukhtar's statue *Nahdat Misr* is finished and erected in Ramses Square, Cairo; it later moved to Cairo University
1952	Free Officers Movement overthrows King Farouk. Egyptian Revolution (also known as the 23 July Revolution) establishes an Egyptian republic and ends the British occupation
1956	General Gamal Abdel Nasser becomes second president of the republic and nationalizes the Suez Canal; after a military confrontation, Britain and France withdraw their forces from Egyptian territory.
1970–81	Presidency of Anwar Sadat; treasures of Tutankhamun tour cities in Europe and the U.S.
1981–2011	Presidency of Hosni Mubarak, ends as a result of the 25 January 2011 revolution

Painted wooden panel with prayers for Tabakenkhonsu, the woman shown wearing a white dress on the right. From Deir el-Bahri, Egypt, *c.* 675 BC. The sky-goddess Nut bends her body over the scene, with her children Isis and Osiris at the left, greeting ibis-headed Thoth.

ONE

LOOKING FOR
ANCIENT EGYPT

I n the early twenty-first century we owe many of our ideas about
memory – and the apparent loss of memory – to the century-
old work of Sigmund Freud. From the consulting room of his
flat in Vienna, Freud formulated ideas that would lead to a significant shift in thinking about the human mind. Freud proposed
that the mind divided into conscious and unconscious operations.
In the unconscious, memories of the past lie buried, not so much
forgotten as suppressed. They motivate our actions, urges and fears
in the present, often in unhelpful ways that could only be overcome by analysing these buried drives. 'Buried' is an apt word here,
because Freud also had a lifelong passion for archaeology – and
that same consulting room was full of images and antiquities
from ancient Greece, Rome and Egypt.[1] Patients like the poet
H. D. reclined on the famous couch beneath a photogravure
depicting the temple of Ramses ii at Abu Simbel by moonlight.
On Freud's desk stood almost three dozen statuettes from ancient
cultures, most of which were cast bronze or carved stone images
of ancient Egyptian gods – like the baboon of Thoth, god of
wisdom, writing and record-keeping. Freud's housekeeper recalled
that he often stroked the smooth head of the stone baboon, like a
favourite pet.

For a book on Egypt in a series called 'Lost Civilizations', the
life and work of Sigmund Freud may seem like a surprising place
to start. Freud's ideas, however, invite us to question how memories are 'lost' not only in individual humans, but in human society
at large. Many academics, philosophers and writers throughout the

twentieth century have explored the idea of a cultural memory that informs the values, structures and daily life of different nations or societies over time.[2] In the United States, for instance, cultural memory could be said to include national celebrations such as Thanksgiving; the canon of American literature, art and architecture, and music; and the horrific experience – and long legacy – of slavery. None of these three is a straightforward memory, given the time that has elapsed and the shared, social way in which cultural memory is held. To take each example in turn, Thanksgiving is a holiday that was created by President Lincoln in 1863 to promote unity during the Civil War, although many Americans assume that it can be traced back to seventeenth-century colonists in New England. As for a 'canon' of the arts, what belongs in or out of any canon is a source of sometimes heated debate. And slavery is pointedly not remembered by American institutions: until the opening of the National Museum of African American Art and Culture in 2016, there was no museum, no memorial, no official recognition at state or national level of the millions who died or endured lives of crippling degradation due to slavery – nor any open acknowledgement of the ongoing impact its slave-owning past has on American society today.

Here is where Freud's theories have seemed to offer insight into the social psyche as well as the individual human mind: buried memories may be suppressing a traumatic event (like slavery), glossing over a history of European colonial incursion, or simply ignoring works that do not easily fit the dominant cultural narrative. Anxiety concentrates around these memories, which are lost but not forgotten. When some trigger – white police shooting unarmed black men, for instance – touches on a painful memory like pressure on a bruise, the trauma reasserts itself in another guise.

If some cultural memories appear to bury difficult histories, what about the shared histories and memories that we seem to celebrate, even revel in? In mainstream Western culture, ancient Egypt often takes this positive role, playing the part of a long-lost civilization that we – the West (problematic as this simplified term is) – have incorporated into our own history and identity. We

Stone baboon owned by Sigmund Freud, made in Egypt or Italy around
the 1st century AD.

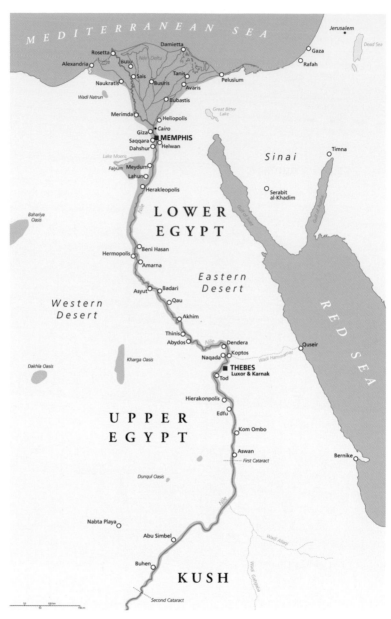

Sites of Ancient Egypt.

'discovered' it, as dozens of books, television shows and museum displays like to put it. And we actively remember it in ways that range from the patriotic, such as the obelisk that dominates the Place de la Concorde in Paris (where the guillotine once stood),[3] to the bombastic, of which the pyramid-shaped Luxor hotel and casino in Las Vegas is just one example.

Is the casino a bit of harmless fun, and is the obelisk merely part of the noble cause of Western science, saving and studying the ancient past for humanity's common good? As this book will show, things are never quite so simple when we try to remember a lost civilization. We will return to France's claims on Egypt later in this book, and to the Las Vegas hotel right at the end, but let us first return to Freud, whose archaeology of the human mind was carried out in tandem with the archaeological discoveries of his day, which Freud followed with an amateur's keen interest. Although he used ancient Greek mythology to characterize his theories and never visited archaeological sites farther from Vienna than Athens and Rome, it was Egypt that occupied his thoughts in later life and Egypt that confronted him as he sat at his desk, face to face with the gods.

Man in the Moon

The baboon still stands in its usual place near the right-hand corner of Freud's desk, arranged in the north London home where he spent the last year of his life, a refugee from Nazi-occupied Vienna. Preserved as the Freud Museum, the house contains the library, antiquities and rug collection (as well as the famous analytic couch) that Freud brought with him in 1938, recreating his familiar surroundings as much as possible in exile. His friend and former patient, Marie Napoléon, paid the tax levy required by the Nazi authorities for all Jewish property taken out of Austria.

Around 21.5 cm (8 in.) high, the statuette represents a male baboon sitting on its haunches, its tail wrapped around its right side and its forepaws on its knees. On its head, a round blob represents the disc of a full moon resting on top of a crescent moon. Although Egyptian in style and subject matter – the baboon was one of two animals identified with Thoth – Freud's figure was probably made in Rome or else in Egypt when it was under Roman imperial rule, from the late first century BC to the third century AD. It is carved from a single piece of marble, a stone rarely found in Egypt but common in Italy and the eastern Mediterranean. The circular base is not typical for Egyptian-style sculpture, which preferred rectangular bases for statues. That, and the fact that the baboon's back paws and the end of its tail have been re-worked where they meet the edge, suggests the Freud baboon has a complex history. It may have been re-carved in modern times from a damaged ancient piece, in order to make it more attractive to someone like Freud, who bought most of his antiquities from the dealer Robert Lustig, owner of a shop near Freud's apartment in Vienna. Egypt and other parts of North Africa and the Middle East had few restrictions on the export of antiquities in the early twentieth century. This meant that there was a steady flow of objects to Europe and beyond – especially small, portable objects that could fit easily into a domestic interior like Freud's. In central Cairo, the new Museum of Egyptian Antiquities that opened in 1902 even had a saleroom where antiquities considered too similar to objects already in the collection, or not important enough, could be bought by members of the public, complete with the required export licence.

The arrangement of figures on Freud's desk suggests he had purposely selected objects that represented ancient learning and wisdom. A highly educated doctor and prolific writer himself, perhaps he looked to figures like the baboon of Thoth, the Greek goddess Athena or the Egyptian wise man Imhotep for inspiration while he worked. In Egyptian mythology Thoth was the god of writing and wisdom. We could argue that Thoth had power over cultural memory and history as well, because as the sacred scribe, it was Thoth who recorded in writing all the key decisions, dates and events that the king and the gods required. He wrote down the outcome of the 'weighing of the heart' that judged the dead, and he inscribed the number of years allotted to a king's reign on the sacred *persea*-tree. Writing mattered in ancient Egypt, where only between 2 and 5 per cent of the populace could read and write. In a population that averaged perhaps 2 million at its height, that amounts to some 40,000 individuals, almost all of them men and boys trained in scribal schools attached to temples. Temples were not just places of ritual and worship: they were the backbone of the Egyptian state and economy. Learning to read and write equipped selected boys for work as scribes, a role that could gain them respect, authority and eventually even a place high up in the country's administration. Boys learned to write by copying out tales with a moralizing bent. One of these school texts advised students, 'love writing more than your mother . . . recognize its beauty, for being a scribe is greater than any profession, and there is nothing else like it on earth.'[4]

His own role as a scribe explains why Thoth often appears in art holding a reed pen, a roll of papyrus and a narrow case to store spare pens and the two ink pots – one black, one red – that every writer needed. Instead of a baboon, Thoth could appear as an African sacred ibis (*Threskiornis aethiopicus*, a wading bird with a thin, curved beak) or, in scenes with other gods, as a human with a healthy male body and an ibis head, supporting the familiar full and crescent moons. This is how he appears in a scene from the *Book of the Dead* papyrus of the well to-do priestess Nestanebtasheru (*c.* 950 BC), which shows Thoth dipping his pen into ink before the falcon-headed god Re-Horakhty.[5] Originally more than 37 metres (121 ft) long, the papyrus was cut into pieces and sandwiched between sheets of glass to help preserve and display it in the British Museum; in antiquity, it formed a thick roll designed to be placed in the priestess's burial. Its hieroglyphic texts take the form of magical spells to help her navigate the underworld. Many of these spells may parallel the arcane wisdom, cult secrets, and entrance or initiation tests that were part of a priest's – or priestess's – working life. Being a priest or priestess brought these individuals into contact with a divine world so powerful that they had to be equipped to deal with it, and in addition to recording the spells and rites they needed, a papyrus like this one represented that other world in all its splendour. Even in black ink on the pure, golden-white papyrus, the lunar disc of Thoth and the sun-disc on the crown of Re-Horakhty represent the light

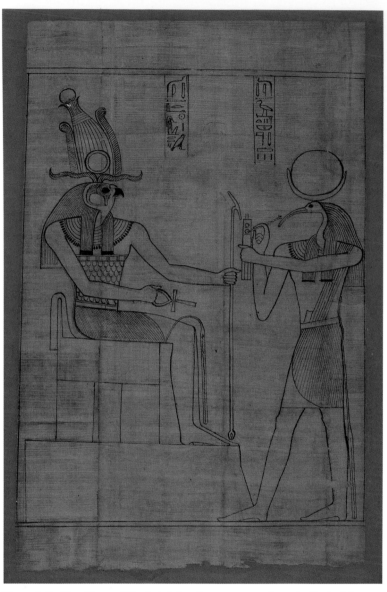

The gods Re-Horakhty and Thoth, ink drawing on papyrus, from the *Book of the Dead* made for the priestess Nestanebtasheru, *c.* 950 BC.

emitted by these heavenly bodies, while the gods' long, streaming hair (what Egyptologists call a three-part, or 'tripartite', wig or headdress) associated them with shining blue skies and rare lapis lazuli. Gods shimmered like gleaming metal and emanated multicoloured sunlight. In Egyptian art, the fact that they are so often made up of human and animal parts – not only their bodies and heads, but the bull tails, bird feathers and animal horns they wear – does not indicate that ancient Egyptians imagined their gods looked like this. These were artistic conventions for showing what could scarcely be imagined, taking elements from the natural world to help picture the ungraspable enormity of the divine.

For a god as significant and as versatile as Thoth, Egyptian artistic conventions meant that his ibis, ibis-headed human and baboon forms all represented 'Thoth', but suited different purposes. Small figures of ibises were popular dedications to Thoth in some periods of Egyptian history, while figures of Thoth as a baboon range from statuettes like Freud's, to tiny amulets, to large, free-standing statues arranged in temple complexes. The animals associated with specific gods were also bred to be sacrificed, mummified and buried as devotional offerings; this practice was widespread from around 600 BC into the Roman period.[6] Near the site of the largest temple of Thoth in Egypt, archaeologists have discovered thousands of mummified ibises and baboons, neatly stacked in catacombs near the human cemetery that served the town.[7] As the god of Egyptian writing and wisdom, Thoth and his cults may have held particular appeal at a time when Egypt came increasingly into contact – and sometimes conflict – with the Assyrian Empire, Greek merchants and mercenaries, and eventually the Roman Empire. With the succession of Egyptian kings disrupted, temples and their priests offered some sense of stability, and Thoth, the gods' own scribe, symbolized a potent mix of writing and wisdom that was increasingly restricted to the literate few who knew the Egyptian scripts and languages. Priests could use their temples as repositories of ancient, secret knowledge while the world around them changed – a strategy that proved to be a success, since it was through the figure of the god Thoth that the classical and medieval worlds remembered the distant past of pharaonic Egypt.

Hermes on the hush

The temple of Thoth, with its vast cemetery of sacred animal mummies, lies on the west bank of the Nile in the province of Al Minya, some 300 km (185 miles) south of Cairo. The names of the archaeological site and adjacent town confirm the long, multi-layered history of ancient Egypt, creating a palimpsest – faint traces of the past that can be glimpsed beneath the modern surface, like erasures that have been written over on a reused piece of parchment. The name of the local town is el-Ashmunein, an Arabic version of an earlier Coptic name, Shmunein, which itself derives from the ancient Egyptian name Khmunu, 'City of the Eight'. In early Egyptian religion, one creation myth held that four pairs of gods, known collectively as 'The Eight', brought the ordered world out of its primeval, watery chaos. Later, as the worship of Thoth became more important in the town, his sacred ibis was added to some versions of the myth. Although gods like Thoth were worshipped throughout Egypt, one of his most important temples was at Khmunu, though hardly any traces of this vast structure survive today.

In Egyptian archaeology, which often uses older place names to refer to ancient sites, el-Ashmunein is better known as Hermopolis, meaning 'city of Hermes' in Greek. As Greek-speaking people from around the eastern Mediterranean began to travel to Egypt for trade, and eventually came to settle in the country after its conquest by Alexander the Great, they drew comparisons between their own gods and the Egyptian gods. This meant that many Egyptian gods could be referred to easily by familiar Greek names, while others – like the Egyptian *Aset* and *Wesir* – were given Greek-style names that we still use (Isis and Osiris in this instance). Today, we most often think of Hermes as the messenger of the Greek gods, equipped with wings to give him speed. But in antiquity Hermes was equally considered a god of language, writing and learning, known for his wit and his wiles. Identifying Hermes with Thoth made linguistic and theological sense, and it was the name Hermopolis that stuck in the imagination of early European visitors, scholars and archaeologists (or Hermopolis Magna,

'The Great', to distinguish it from a smaller Egyptian town of the same name).

It was not only Greeks visiting or living in Egypt who took an interest in Egyptian religion. Extensive trade links throughout the eastern Mediterranean – the coasts of Egypt, the Levant and Turkey; the islands of Cyprus, Crete and the Aegean Sea; and the Italian peninsula – had been facilitated by Greek and Phoenician (from Lebanon) sailors for many years. Small Egyptian cult centres flourished from at least the second century BC, and probably earlier, into the Roman Empire. The religion practised in the Mediterranean centred on the goddess Isis, the sister-wife of the mythical king Osiris, who used her powerful magic to restore his life force (and sexual potency) after his brother Seth murdered him. Isis was an all-powerful mother figure, conceiving a son, Horus, by the dead Osiris and raising the child in secret until he was old enough to avenge his father.

The Isis cult celebrated in the Mediterranean world also incorporated many Egyptian ideas related to the Nile flood, the river's holy water and the worship of sacred animals. In Italy, the towns of Pompeii and Herculaneum, which were buried by the eruption of Mount Vesuvius in AD 79, both had temples dedicated to Isis and focused on Egyptian cult.[8] A surviving wall painting from Herculaneum represents a ceremony in progress at just such an Isis temple. Consisting of a small sanctuary with a central doorway, which stands on a platform reached by several steps, the sanctuary in the Herculaneum painting is quite unlike any traditional Egyptian temple (like the temple of Thoth at Hermopolis), but it resembles the basic structure of Isis shrines built in both Italy and Egypt during the first and second centuries AD. The Herculaneum painting suggests a certain exoticism, with palm trees and sphinxes either side of the temple. African sacred ibises, with their distinctive black-and-white plumage, perch on a tall altar to the right of the painting, and, in front of a shorter altar in the foreground, one priest fans the flames of the burnt offerings while another holds a palm frond, like a fan. Several figures in the crowd of worshippers brandish the metal rattle known as a *sistrum* (plural, *sistra*), an ancient Egyptian percussion instrument that made a rhythmic *sh-sh-sh*-sound considered pleasing to the gods – hence its ancient Egyptian onomatopoeic name, *shesheshet*. The priest and priestess nearest the sphinxes also hold *sistra*, while the priest at the foot of the temple steps brandishes a narrow feather, in an echo of the feathers that feature so prominently in Egyptian art.

Last but far from least, the priest who stands in front of the temple doorway cradles a special vessel, with a pouring spout, which was used to hold water for ritual washing. Notice how he has wrapped his hands in the folds of his robe, so that his skin makes no contact with the sacred water pitcher. As in many religions, ideas about purity and cleanliness were important in

Wall painting from a villa at Herculaneum, Italy, 1st century AD.

Egyptian practice, whether 'at home' in Egypt or in cults based elsewhere. While they were on duty, Egyptian priests wore fresh linen garments, abstained from certain foods and sexual practices, and shaved their body hair, which explains why the painting depicts the male ritualists as bald-headed. It was men like these (priestesses seem to have played different roles, or been sidelined) who kept alive the writings, rituals and religious concepts that they believed had been handed down over many generations from earlier priests. And like those generations of priests before them, they characterized their knowledge as a secret, revealed only to themselves and select initiates who were trained up in ways that would keep these secrets safe.

Because Thoth, and his Greek analogue in Hermes, was the most venerable god of writing and wisdom, the figure of Thoth/Hermes came to symbolize the totality of what was known about the mysteries of the cosmos and of human nature – what we would now be likely to refer to as science and philosophy. Presenting this knowledge as a secret does not mean that there really was a particular secret involved, or any of the wizardry some people attribute to ancient Egypt today. In any society, secrets offer a powerful form of social influence. Those who are in on the secret may have access to restricted spaces, networks and supplies (like a private members' club); this not only helps them guard their own privileges, but demonstrate those privileges to everyone who is outside the enclave. There is little point in having a secret unless someone knows you have it: in this way, secrets are surprisingly public, however paradoxical that seems.

In the transmission of Egyptian religion to the Greek and Roman worlds, secrecy increasingly came to be seen as a hallmark of Egypt's gods and the specialist know-how of its priests – whether that entailed reading and writing hieroglyphs (from the Greek for 'sacred signs') or indulging in the sort of mystical speculations typical of the many small cults that flourished under the Roman Empire and into Late Antiquity, even as Christianity gained a firm foothold. From the name of Hermes we derive the word 'hermetic', to describe something that is secret and sealed off from the rest of society. And it was in the form of Hermes – specifically, Hermes the Three-times Great ('Trismegistus', a translation of the Egyptian *wer wer wer*) – that the Egyptian Thoth found his way into the European imagination. As Hermes Trismegistus, Thoth was the legendary author of several philosophical manuals preserved in Greek, but partly inspired by Egyptian models and written in their most recent form between the first and third centuries AD.[9] Known as the *Corpus Hermeticum*, these texts were lost (that word again) to the western, Latin-speaking Roman empire until their rediscovery during the Italian Renaissance, although they had survived in forms that were familiar to the Greek, Coptic, Syriac and eventually Arabic-speaking east. Across the cultural gulf that had opened between Christian Europe and the Islamic Middle East, the figure of Hermes Trismegistus held out the promise of ancient wisdom that could be put to new use in the early modern era.

From Siena to Vienna

A Roman Catholic cathedral may be the last place anyone expects to encounter an ancient Egyptian god – but the spectacular floor of the Cathedral of St Catherine in Siena places Hermes Trismegistus in pride of place, just across the threshold of the nave. The cathedral's floor was created between the fourteenth and sixteenth centuries, each panel designed by a leading artist and executed in white, black, red and green marbles, using the intarsia technique whereby large pieces of stone were cut to shape and laid together in tight joins. The panel depicting Hermes Trismegistus, the medieval version of Thoth, was designed by sculptor Giovanni di Stefano in 1488.[10] In keeping with other depictions of Hermes Trismegistus around this time, he appears in the guise of a bearded sage. His tall, pointed hat marks him out as an Eastern priest or wise man (it was modelled on depictions of one of the last Byzantine emperors), and his heavy robes hint at ancient styles of dress, touched with the luxurious yellow of gold. The Latin inscription at the bottom of the mosaic panel can be translated as 'Hermes Mercury Trismegistus, contemporary of Moses': the biblical prophet, who was himself born and raised in Egypt, also represented Egyptian wisdom in the minds of educated Renaissance viewers. In fifteenth-century Europe there was nothing strange about associating Hermes Trismegistus, a 'pagan' figure, with the leader of the biblical Exodus. Ancient philosophers like Plato were avidly read and admired in learned circles, their views on the nature of the world taken to be just as illuminating as the books of the Bible when it came to understanding the origins of Christian thought. As the presumed author of the *Corpus Hermeticum*, copies of which had been rediscovered in Italy in the 1460s, Hermes Trismegistus was another source of wisdom, and specifically Egyptian wisdom – the most ancient and effective kind.

The Siena pavement makes the Egyptian identity of Hermes Trismegistus clear – not in its style or decorative elements, as we might expect, but in the Latin words written across the book he holds open: *Suscipite o lecteras et leges Egipti* (Take up letters and laws, O Egyptians!). The two figures on the left, one of whom supports the book, probably represent the Egyptians whom Hermes is urging towards literacy and the rule of law. Certainly the man supporting the book, who leans eagerly towards the sage, has a certain non-European appearance, thanks to his wide turban and short beard. On the other side of Hermes Trismegistus, a table supported by Greek-style sphinxes also refers to secret wisdom, sacred words and God the creator, beloved of his son; its Latin inscription quotes one of the *Corpus Hermeticum* texts. With Hermes as its central axis, the mosaic panel thus uses both image and text to suggest a direct relationship between ancient Egypt's skilled writings and the promise of creation, ultimately fulfilled, in Christian thought, by the birth of Jesus Christ. The triangle formed by Hermes' pointed hat and his outstretched arms is the visual link between the pre-Christian past and the Christian present of fifteenth-century Italy.

Did the faithful of Siena recognize these allusions when they entered the Cathedral on their way to Mass? Very few would have had the sophisticated level of learning required to understand the image or the text, just as few tourists (or readers) today are familiar with Hermes Trismegistus at all – and they would be surprised to learn that he is Egyptian when the pavement lacks any motifs that we would now consider Egyptian. No pyramid, no winged sun

The sage Hermes
Trismegistus,
in the stone floor
of the cathedral
of Siena, Italy, 1488.

disc and no hieroglyphs, for a start. The path from the *Book of the Dead* created in around 1000 BC, to Freud's baboon sculpted around AD 100, and from the Herculaneum painting of perhaps 100 BC to the Siena pavement in the late fifteenth century, seems to retreat from the Egyptian sources in visual style, as if the artists of ancient Rome and Renaissance Italy had forgotten what the ibis-headed god and his baboon alter ego should look like. And in a sense, they had: over the course of the Middle Ages (roughly around the sixth to mid-fifteenth centuries AD), political, social and religious changes throughout Europe and the Middle East meant that there was little direct contact between Egypt and western Europe. Until the seventeenth century European ideas about ancient Egyptian art mostly derived from obelisks, sculptures and small antiquities that had been imported to Italy in Roman times or created by Roman artists in an Egyptian style. As we have seen, European ideas about ancient Egyptian religion had also been filtered through Greek and Latin sources, many of which emphasized the venerability of Egyptian wisdom alongside its hidden, almost mystical, nature.

In eighteenth-century Europe the cultural shift known as the Enlightenment began to change the way Europeans thought about Egypt, both ancient and modern. Often idealized as an 'age of reason' and an era of discovery, the Enlightenment must also be seen within the political and economic contexts that made it possible, including colonialism, industrialization and the slave trade. European expansionism, backed by military power, created the conditions in which explorers and merchants began to travel to Egypt, record their impressions, and bring curiosities, like animal mummies and *shabti*-figures, back home with them. Throughout this time period, the notion persisted that ancient Egypt was a place of both mystery and enlightenment. Secret societies like the Freemasons and the Rosicrucians, whose structures, iconography and teachings were inspired by Hermetic thought, held an appeal for men from the expanding middle classes and more 'enlightened' corners of the aristocracy. They tapped into old ideas as well as new needs for meeting spaces where the revolutionary issues of the day could be debated and social alliances forged. Freemasonry was famously celebrated in Mozart's 1791 opera *The Magic Flute*, whose hero finds redemption in romantic love and, more importantly, in a Romantic encounter with the wisdom of the ancient past, revealed by the magician-priest Sarastro. In the opera's closing scene, the chorus sings its praises to Isis and Osiris – a triumph of light over darkness, and of knowledge over wisdom.

As we will see in the next chapter, Napoleon Bonaparte's 1798 expedition to Egypt is usually cited as a watershed in the modern European encounter with ancient Egyptian civilization, because it brought fresh accounts of the country, its antiquities and its contemporary culture to the attention of the West. It also opened trade and diplomatic channels between Western powers and Mohamed Ali, the Albanian-born military leader who emerged to govern Egypt on behalf of the Ottoman Sultan. No single event, but a series of developments and cultural dialogues, saw ancient Egypt become a subject of dedicated academic study over the course of the nineteenth century. Museums and the commercial trade in antiquities boomed as well, and by the outbreak of the First World War in 1914, nearly every city in Europe and North America could boast some kind of display of ancient Egyptian art, and perhaps even a local landmark designed in Egyptian style. This was the background against which Freud purchased his Thoth baboon in a Viennese shop. Within walking distance of his Vienna apartment,

Freud could – and did – marvel at the prestigious Egyptian collection of the Kunsthistorisches (Art History) Museum, complete with an Egyptian-themed mural by Gustav Klimt. The secrets of Egypt were within such easy reach, and were so well studied, that they hardly seemed secret at all.

Yet there was a darker side to this tale of enlightenment. Archaeology in Egypt went hand-in-hand with colonial efforts to create and control the Suez Canal, industrialize cotton production and bring the Sudan under British imperial sway. Separating the remains of ancient Egypt from the country's contemporary population was one way in which Western culture kept the 'discovery' of Egypt's past to itself, in the literal form of museum objects and tourist sites as well as imaginative forms such as literature, music, drama and the arts. In the shifting geopolitical landscape that emerged after the First World War, with the break-up of the Ottoman Empire, serious challenges to this one-sided approach began to emerge. In the 1920s and 1930s Egyptian leaders asserted their independence as a nation state, a process that often evoked ancient Egyptian civilization as a proud precedent for self-rule in the face of Western racism and mockery.[11] Outside Egypt but at the same time, descendants of the African diaspora also demanded greater recognition in societies like the United States, where African Americans had so long been disenfranchised by the legacy of slavery. Writers and artists in the Harlem Renaissance articulated their hopes for a better future, and their despair for the present, with reference to ancient Egypt, which came to represent the possibility of recovering a lost African homeland and remaking a fairer world in its image.

Nor did the mysticism associated with Thoth and Hermes Trismegistus ever entirely go away, as any Internet search soon shows us. Esoteric approaches to ancient Egyptian civilization found a ready home in Britain around the turn of the twentieth century and again between the two world wars, offering an alternative to conventional religion and promoting an anti-establishment view whereby ancient, 'primitive' cultures were considered to be more 'authentic' than the modern world. In the late 1930s the occultist Aleister Crowley, who once claimed to be a reincarnated

Egyptian priest, devised a pack of Tarot cards that he called *The Book of Thoth*, replete with elaborate associations between alchemy, astrology, Egyptian mythology and Chinese divination. Crowley was a notorious fantasist and manipulator, who alienated all but a few loyal followers. His interest in ancient Egyptian magic and mysticism stretched back to the 1890s, when he attended meetings of a Rosicrucian-inspired secret society called the Hermetic Order of the Golden Dawn, which met in bohemian Bloomsbury and counted among its members W. B. Yeats and Olivia Shakespear.[12] Ancient Egypt, as ever, made strange bedfellows.

A world away from Crowley's fantastical rehashings, but in the same zeitgeist of a Europe sliding inexorably towards war, Sigmund Freud settled into his new home in London, patted the baboon of Thoth on its head, and finished writing his revisionist, psychoanalytic history *Moses and Monotheism*.[13] In this final work, Freud used his theories of suppressed memory to argue that the biblical leader Moses was not Jewish but an Egyptian, and that the worship of a single god that made Judaism such a distinctive religion had its origin in the murder of the Egyptian king Akhenaten, who had promoted monotheism over the objections of the old priesthood. This controversial book seems to have been Freud's way of addressing his own complex feelings about religion and identity (raised in a secular Jewish household, he was an atheist), at a time when National Socialism posed an ever-growing threat to European Jews. What a weight the little marble baboon and its desktop companions had to bear.

Why Sigmund Freud chose to keep an image of Thoth on his desk, only Freud himself could know. But tracing the lineage of this god from his worship in ancient Egypt to his appeal in the Roman world, and from his Renaissance existence as Hermes Trismegistus to his legacy in the twentieth-century occult, gives us a sense of the many and varied purposes to which ancient Egyptian civilization has been put over the past two thousand years. Like human memory, cultural memory always has gaps – areas of forgetfulness that accrue over time, as well as knowledge that is 'lost' when it becomes convenient to do so, for example when a language is no longer considered worth speaking or when images of gods are destroyed because new gods have taken their place. Which groups of people claim to have 'found' ancient Egypt (and why) is a question we will return to again and again in this book. There is no right or wrong way to think about history, especially a history as far removed from us today as the history of ancient Egypt. But evaluating what we think we know, how we know it, and why we care in the first place, is a good place to start – and so we will.

TWO
FORTY CENTURIES

The French painter Antoine-Jean Gros knew exactly which side his baguette was buttered on. Trained in the studio of Jacques-Louis David (the painter par excellence of the French Revolution and its aftermath, and himself a canny politician), Gros befriended the future empress Josephine de Beauharnais and earned Napoleon's trust as a painter loyal to the French army.[1] His monumental paintings of Napoleon's military exploits won acclaim at the biennial Salons held in Paris during the years when Napoleon was consolidating his power, initially as First Consul and from 1804 as self-proclaimed emperor. At a time when state sponsorship and oversight of the arts meant that large-scale projects had to function as propaganda, Gros managed to exercise his considerable artistic talent in the genre of history painting, even if his subject matter inevitably portrayed Napoleon in a sympathetic – or sycophantic – light.

Completed in 1810 and displayed in the palace of Versailles, Gros' oil painting *The Battle of the Pyramids* is one of his smaller works, at almost 4 metres long. It was popular enough to be engraved for sale as prints. The canvas typifies the aggrandizing visual narratives of Napoleon's 1798 campaign in the Middle East, a campaign that had ended in defeat a decade earlier, but which lived on in the French national imagination. At the time he had set out on the expedition, Napoleon Bonaparte was an ambitious young general, steeped in accounts of ancient history, such as the career of Alexander the Great, but equally familiar with current thinking in civil engineering and military strategy. For some time

Antoine-Jean Gros, *The Battle of the Pyramids*, 1810, oil on canvas.

engineers had reasoned that it would be possible to dig a shorter seafaring route through the Suez isthmus, just east of the Sinai peninsula, and thus join the Mediterranean and the Red Sea. Such a shipping route would cut weeks off the journey from Europe to the Indian Ocean and allow France to challenge Britain's lucrative colonization of the Indian subcontinent. Napoleon sailed from France on 19 May 1798, with 35,000 soldiers and 167 specialists known as the savants, or scholars: engineers, chemists, mineralogists, botanists, zoologists and draughtsmen, including the artist, author, diplomat and sometime spy Vivant-Dominique Denon, who would prove pivotal in bringing the antiquities of Egypt to much greater attention in Europe. Denon was also pivotal in Gros' career: once they were back in Paris, Napoleon made Denon director of the art museum in the Louvre.[2] This also gave Denon the task of organizing the Salons and encouraging French artists to create paintings suited to the new age of empire, which increasingly meant showing Napoleon's kinder, gentler side.

In 1801 French troops abandoned Egypt after a series of defeats on land and sea, routed by Britain's navy and Ottoman forces; since Napoleon's fleet had been destroyed, British ships transported the 19,000 surviving French troops home. Napoleon himself had returned to France already in 1799, to stage a *coup d'état*, but he preferred to be commemorated in paint as caretaker of his troops and of the nation, more an inspiring hero than a marauding crusader. That is the guise in which Gros portrays him in *The Battle of the Pyramids*, a painting that does not try accurately to depict this opening battle of July 1798 but instead combines historical reality (portraits of Napoleon and his officers) with the allegorical motifs of conquest and clemency: a fallen black soldier, understood at the time as Ethiopian, lies dead, while two men representing Arab and Turkish soldiers beg Napoleon for mercy. Napoleon's declamatory arm gesture aligns him with the grandeur of the pyramids and marks the moment before the battle when he addressed his troops, allegedly urging them on with the words, 'Soldiers, from these monuments forty centuries of history look down on you!' It was quite a gauntlet to throw down to his men, especially given that they were wearing wool uniforms under the sweltering Egyptian sun and facing severe shortages of food and water. They managed a decisive victory nonetheless, forcing the forces of Egypt's Mamluk rulers to withdraw and regroup. This auspicious opening of the campaign made it a perfect subject for

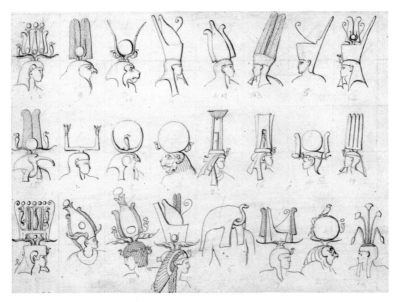

Dominique Vivant Denon, drawings based on temple scenes at Philae, Egypt, *c.* 1802.

Gros, even though everyone visiting the Salon in 1810 knew the victory had been short-lived.

Why did Napoleon think the pyramids represented 4,000 years of history? A more accurate estimate would be 4,500 years, as it turns out, but his round-number 'guesstimate' was not far off. What did an educated European like Napoleon know about the ancient Egyptian past in 1798, and how does anyone calculate the years and epochs of 'history', anyway? As we saw in Chapter One, ideas about ancient Egypt have always changed depending on which people, in which time period, have a vested interest in its culture, from ancient Rome, to medieval Cairo, to early 1900s Vienna. In this chapter, we step back to consider how the chronology of ancient Egyptian history has been pieced together over time, including some of the debates it has inspired. Given the pressure Napoleon's soldiers were already under, perhaps it is just as well their leader failed to realize that more than forty centuries had gone into the making of Egyptian history before his hero, Alexander the Great, had even been born.

Joseph's granaries

The survey of ancient Egypt outlined in this chapter, from prehistory to the seventh century AD, presents evidence currently available from the work of archaeologists and Egyptologists. It is a conventional academic history, a best guess at asserting what happened and when. There are other ways of telling the history of ancient Egypt, in what are often described as 'alternative' approaches. Some people believe that ancient Egypt was settled by survivors from the lost utopia of Atlantis described by Plato, or that the pyramids were built with help from extraterrestrial life. But there have been other histories within what we would consider rational scientific approaches, as well: in seventeenth-century Europe several scholars, including Johannes Kepler, Isaac Newton and, most influentially, Archbishop James Ussher, used year-spans given in the Bible to calculate that God had created the world in 4004 BC. Even in the twentieth century some fundamentalist Christians still accepted that the world was only a few millennia old, not the billions of years demonstrated by the work of geologists and palaeontologists over the course of the nineteenth century. During the 1925 Scopes Trial in Tennessee, for instance, leading American politician and anti-evolution campaigner William Jennings Bryan consulted Ussher's chronology to argue that the biblical flood occurred only in 2348 BC, an argument for which he was lampooned in the press, but which reflected sincerely held beliefs.

If Napoleon did think the pyramids had been built forty centuries before 1798, his rhetoric made use of what Europeans then knew about ancient history. At this time European scholars relied on the accounts of the few travellers who had visited Egypt, plus translations from Arabic authors and ancient Greek and Roman writers. The three pyramids at Giza inspired a lengthy discussion in the Greek traveller Herodotus, whose work had been well known in Europe since the Renaissance. Herodotus visited Egypt in the fifth century BC, speaking to Egyptian priests – or, through translators, other local residents – for information about the country's history and monuments.[3] Much of what Herodotus reported would later be confirmed by Egyptologists, such as the names of the kings who built the pyramids – Cheops (Khufu, in Egyptian), Chephren (Khafre) and Mycerinos (Menkaure) – and the fact that the structures have no subterranean chambers. Until copies of Herodotus were rediscovered in fifteenth-century Italy and translated into Latin, however, Europeans associated the pyramids with the Old Testament story of Joseph. Sold by his jealous brothers into slavery in Egypt, Joseph became the Egyptian pharaoh's most trusted adviser, thanks to his intelligence and God's favour. According to the Book of Genesis, Joseph predicted a period of low Nile floods and convinced the Egyptians to stockpile enough grain to ward off famine. In medieval Europe the giant stone structures said to stand in the desert outside Cairo were thus known as Joseph's granaries and represented as barn-like structures in the thirteenth-century calfskin map of the world preserved in Hereford Cathedral.[4] Surely structures so ancient and so monumental must refer to biblical events?

In the medieval Arab world the pyramids of Giza made similarly grand impressions on writers like Abd el-Latif al-Baghdadi, a thirteenth-century author who explored and measured the Giza pyramids, commented on their alignment with each other and the close fit of their masonry blocks, and weighed up arguments for their age, concluding that they pre-dated the great flood that both the Quran and the Bible record. Al-Baghdadi had the advantage of being on the ground in Egypt, where it was obvious to him that the pyramids were tombs (for revered prophets, he thought) situated within a vast cemetery. He also knew that they had been a focus of pilgrimage for millennia, and al-Baghdadi took them as clear indications of the 'noble intellects' of the ancient people who had built them.[5] Arabic scholars of the thirteenth century were better informed than their European counterparts about ancient Egyptian history – yet today it is Herodotus, not al-Baghdadi, who is quoted in every survey of Egyptian civilization, or name-checked in television documentaries. It is worth remembering that the weight we give to different sources of evidence does not necessarily correspond to the innate value of that evidence. Instead, cultural bias creeps into research that academics, like all scientists, have been eager to present as objective, fair and balanced. No research takes place in a vacuum, however; every scholar writes at a certain historical juncture, using the sources available at the time.

During the reign of Napoleon, a French translation of al-Baghdadi's work was published by the leading specialist in Arabic and other 'Oriental' languages (as they were known), Antoine Silvestre de Sacy. Herodotus, however, already had the upper hand; his much older work, composed in Greek, was considered to be more European and hence more reliable (or at least, more quotable) a source than the more recent Arabic writings of al-Baghdadi. As the powerful nation states of western Europe eyed up the financial and military benefits they stood to gain in North Africa and the Middle East, the 'Oriental' populations who lived there became more detached – in European eyes – from the ancient past of the region, whose roots in the biblical and Classical worlds seemed to make it European by default. Such Orientalism, as literary critic Edward Said dubbed it in his 1978 book of the same name, allowed the West to imagine an East ripe for the picking.[6] What was at stake in the Battle of the Pyramids was a land grab, to be sure.

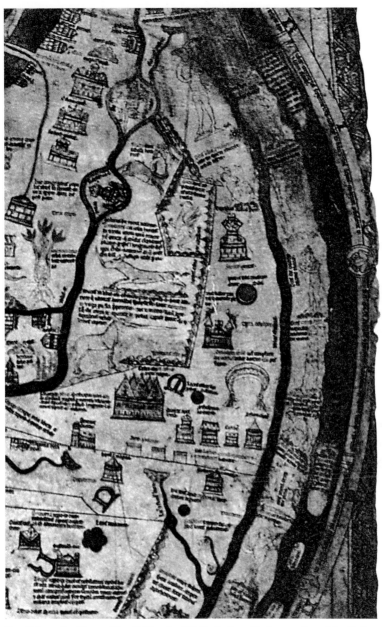

Detail from the *Mappa Mundi*, Hereford Cathedral – with the crossing of the Red Sea at top left and the Nile to the right.

But the work of Napoleon's savants, and the early Egyptologists who followed them, sought to grab intellectual territory, too: the pyramids, and all they represented about an ancient Egypt where Europe's own glorious roots might lie.

Writing history: king lists, chronologies and the myth of civilization

In the nineteenth century, Europeans often used the word 'Oriental' to refer to anyone living between Morocco and Turkey, in a great sweep around the southern and eastern Mediterranean. These societies were backwards and underdeveloped in comparison to European culture, ran the argument, and historians of the time characterized different civilizations as if they were living organisms, with a moment of birth, growth and inevitable death. This 'rise and fall' motif unhelpfully still informs the way we speak about history today.

As a better understanding of ancient Egyptian history emerged over the course of the nineteenth century, the idea of a 'rise and fall' was built into the structure of its chronology. Eras of the most extensive royal power were dubbed the Old, Middle and New Kingdoms (see the Chronology at the start of this book), while the centuries in between became known as Intermediate Periods, as if time were simply ticking along until something interesting happened. To historians of the nineteenth century, steeped in the idea of a nation state with a stable population bounded by territory, only 'native' rule was legitimate in a sovereign country. Hence the conventional narrative of Egyptian history charts a long decline beginning in the eighth century BC, when rulers from the kingdom of Kush, in what is now Sudan, conquered Egypt after a series of skirmishes with Assyrian forces from present-day Iraq. For the next three hundred years or so, Egypt was governed successively by the Kushite kings, the Assyrian Empire and the Persian Empire (based in modern Iran), with interludes when kings who identified themselves as Egyptian reasserted control. By 332 BC, when Napoleon's hero Alexander the Great was stepping up his campaign against Persia, Egypt was a satellite of Persia with little or no central government of its own. Many Egyptians seem to have welcomed Alexander and the Macedonian Greek rulers who followed him, turning the country into a Hellenistic kingdom until the death of Cleopatra in 30 BC ceded it to Roman rule.

From this period of so-called 'decline', however, came the source that modern historians relied on for the framework of ancient Egyptian chronology still used today, with its division into 31 (now usually shortened to 30) dynasties of human kings: the *Aegyptiaca,* or *Egyptian Matters,* a history of Egypt written by an Egyptian priest named Manetho in the early third century BC.[7] Like many Egyptians of his status at that time, Manetho was fluent in both Egyptian and Greek, the language in which he wrote his history. He lived during the reigns of Egypt's new family of Macedonian kings, Ptolemy I Soter (who had been a childhood companion and colleague of Alexander) and his son Ptolemy II Philadelphus. Although no complete text of Manetho's history survives, it was quoted extensively in other Greek and Latin histories. These excerpts tell us that Manetho was a priest in major Egyptian temples at Heliopolis, near Cairo, and at Sebennytos in the Delta. He was familiar not only with Egyptian religion and literature, but with Greek mythology and Greek writers like Herodotus, whose own history writing provided a model for Manetho. Being a priest gave Manetho access to temple records, from inscribed walls and stelae (upright stone slabs) to libraries full of papyrus scrolls dating back generations, if not centuries. Here, Manetho wrote, were the sacred books and records he translated to narrate the succession of Egyptian kings from a long-distant period of rule by gods and demigods to the Persian kings who immediately preceded Alexander's conquest, and whose reigns Manetho counted as the 31st Dynasty, a tactic scholars have since abandoned.

Based on his research into temple records, Manetho assigned a certain number of years of rule to each king he named, tallying the total years for each dynasty as he went along. Counting by reign lengths was the standard way of marking time in ancient Egypt and in many other past cultures. Rather than starting from a fixed date – the Exodus, the birth of Christ, the *hejira* – as the Jewish, Christian and Muslim calendars do, ancient Egyptian calendars

Seti I and his son, the future Ramses II, with a list of Egyptian kings, Abydos, Egypt, *c.* 1275 BC.

started fresh with each new king. Instead of writing 2016, for instance, an ancient Egyptian priest would record the 65th year of Queen Elizabeth II, counting from her ascension. To have a longer perspective, it was important to keep track of kings' reign lengths in their order of rule.[8] These king lists survive on papyrus and in stone inscriptions, such as the list carved on a temple wall at the sacred city of Abydos in southern Egypt. In a neatly ruled grid, carefully spaced equidistant from each other, oval rings (called cartouches) encircle the name of each ruler. In addition to papyrus documents, inscriptions like these are the kinds of sources Manetho had access to in writing his history. The artistry and scale of the Abydos king list, which filled an entire corridor in the temple, are a sign not only of its usefulness as a historical record, but, and even more so, of its importance in forming and maintaining social memory in ancient Egypt: social forgetting, too, since it left out rulers later deemed heretical, such as Hatshepsut, a queen who ruled as if she were a king in her own right. The months, if not years, it took to design, carve and paint such lists, which existed in temples up and down the country, reinforced the unity of Egypt for everyone involved, from the priests and sculptors to the temple bakers and cleaners.

Communal acts of commemoration help societies create and recreate themselves across generations, and in a society like ancient Egypt, which maintained a stable, core identity for several millennia, the celebration of kingship in art, myth and ritual helped make that possible. Even Egypt's 'foreign' kings, like the Ptolemies under whom Manetho lived, contributed to this coherent historical narrative by styling themselves as Egyptian pharaohs when the situation warranted. Rather than a 'decline', these centuries that saw Egypt enmeshed ever more closely with neighbouring cultures could instead be seen as an era of transformation and creative hybridity.

Nor was cross-cultural contact anything new: no culture exists in isolation. Historians of the nineteenth and early twentieth centuries tended to think in terms of 'types' or 'races' of peoples who developed in bounded geographic locations and displayed certain character traits: the cool and calculating East Asian, the despotic Oriental, the rational European and the primitive African or

Aboriginal. Although these essentialist categories have long been debunked, their stereotypes lurk just under the surface of contemporary society, and the idea that a group 'belongs' to one, delimited territory, has proved difficult to shake. The movement of people, raw materials and finished products is as old as human society itself. Arguably, contact and exchange made civilization happen, if by 'civilization' we mean the development of larger-scale settlements, more complex technologies and more stratified social structures. What 'civilization' should not imply, however, is a superior way of living: every society on any scale, and whether settled, nomadic or a bit of both, has its own intricate ways of doing and being. Those same historians who assumed that there were 'types' of people also assumed that there was a sliding scale of cultural development, from the primitive (literally, the first or earliest human cultures) to the most 'civilized' or 'advanced' societies of the modern age. However, social evolutionism like this was problematic: 'primitive' stood both for a chronologically early stage of human development and for contemporary human groups considered to be 'backwards' in comparison to the Western specialists who studied them. In the rise and fall approach to history, some cultures seemed never to get off the ground, or to have almost nothing in common with the cultures that came after them, in the same territory. How to reconcile a 'civilized' society with its 'primitive' origins challenged modern and ancient historians alike.

Forty centuries BC

At the other end of the timeline from the eras of Kushite, Persian and Ptolemaic rule stands a period that Egyptologists today refer to as the Predynastic: before the invention of writing, and before the dynasties of human kings named in Manetho's *Aegyptiaca*. Manetho himself dealt with this distant past in a way that was typical for ancient Egyptian and Greek writers: he attributed thousands of years after the world's creation to the rule of gods and demigods. Without written records to the contrary, who could argue? Besides which, gods and demigods were appropriate forebears for the lines of kings that followed.

In the late nineteenth century archaeologists took up the challenge of how to identify, assign dates to and interpret the prehistoric sites they began to find in Egypt. Research on this era continues to be an important and evolving focus of archaeology in Egypt today.[9] Cemeteries preserved in the desert fringes, either side of the fertile Nile flood plain, have been the primary sources of information about the early agricultural and pastoral societies that occupied the Nile Delta, the Fayum depression and the Valley between around 5000 and 3000 BC. During this period, which corresponds to the Neolithic (stone age) and Chalcolithic (copperstone age), the Egyptian landscape supported more grassland, but over time a desert climate prevailed, encouraging groups of people to settle closer to the flood plain, although some will still have moved from place to place with herds of grazing animals.

The prolific British archaeologist W. M. Flinders Petrie conducted one of the first major excavations of a Predynastic cemetery, found in 1894 near the site of Naqada in southern Egypt. Bodies were buried on their sides, knees bent, and were often wrapped in basketry mats and sometimes resin-soaked linen textiles, too. Their graves included items such as stone and pottery vessels, stone palettes for grinding cosmetic pigment, carnelian and quartz beads, flint and obsidian tools, and minerals like galena and malachite. Many of these objects are evidence of wide-ranging trade connections (obsidian from Ethiopia, mineral ores from the neighbouring mountain ranges and Sinai, shells from the Red Sea) and technological mastery, for instance in textile and pottery production. The distribution of objects in burials suggests social differentiation in terms of who was buried with certain object types or treatments of the body. At the site of Hierakonpolis, for instance, archaeologists recently discovered the body of a woman whose limbs had been wrapped in the fragrant bark of the *Boswellia* tree, better known as frankincense and probably imported from Somalia or Ethiopia.[10] The Nile was essential not only for its annual flood, which deposited rich silt for agriculture, but as a means of transport. From around 3500 BC decorated pottery began to appear in graves, often adorned with pictures of many-oared boats. Some scholars have suggested that the figures or symbols depicted on

Painted pottery jar from Egypt, c. 3400 BC.

these boats – here, birds near one end and humans above (perhaps inside?) two central cabins – represent deities, which might link these Predynastic pots to Egyptian myths in which gods and kings sail through a celestial version of the Nile. But whether we can project later religious ideas backwards in time is open to question. Myths and other cultural forms from the historic era can suggest possible interpretations, but there is no single, secure answer about what these objects meant to their ancient makers.

In studying Predynastic Egypt scholars also look forward in time, as the very name 'Predynastic' indicates: it anticipates the Dynastic period, which starts with Manetho's 1st Dynasty and marks a point at which the Nile Valley and Delta became united under a single king. Since the 1980s scholars have also added a stage in between called the 'Protodynastic', or Dynasty 0. During this period of state formation, a shared organizational structure emerged, coordinating large-scale temples, extensive trade links and centralized resources. These new, early kings and their supporters formed an influential upper stratum of society and accordingly needed forms of art, architecture and personal adornment to help set themselves apart and maintain the upper hand. Within only one or two generations, it seems, the first king of the first recorded dynasty – Manetho called him Menes, scholars today think he was Narmer – flipped a cultural switch: the older forms of pottery decoration and palette carving disappeared, and in their place came monumental mud-brick tombs, the invention of hieroglyphic writing and a fresh artistic style that would be recognizable for millennia to come. Most of the kings of Manetho's first two dynasties were buried in vast, mound-like, mud-brick complexes in the southern city of Abydos, but by the 3rd Dynasty these mounds gave way to pyramids, a form that could only be fit for a king.

Pyramid ages

The first Egyptian pyramids were not the famous trio at Giza, towards which Napoleon gestures in Gros' *Battle of the Pyramids*. Instead, the more humble origins of the pyramid form, and the many ways in which it was later deployed, chart a timeline of Egyptian culture more complex than any 'rise and fall' narrative could suggest.[11]

The three Giza pyramids, which date from the 4th Dynasty of the Old Kingdom, are justly famous for their immense size and because they look like pyramids: four straight, triangular sides leaning in from a square base. Of the dozens of royal pyramids that once dotted the Nile Valley, most had a similar form but have rarely survived to their full height, especially where fine-quality stone casing the exterior was taken for reuse, or where hastier construction methods proved less impervious to time. The first pyramids were not 'true' pyramids at all but tiered layers, such as the Step Pyramid of king Djoser at Saqqara. Constructed during his long reign in the 3rd Dynasty, Djoser's pyramid was remembered in later Egyptian history as an innovation by the priest Imhotep, a historical figure who was worshipped as a demigod after his death. Revered for his wisdom and, in particular, his medical skill, the link between Imhotep and the Step Pyramid suggests that this monument endured in Egypt's cultural memory: in the Late Period, local people made new burials within the vicinity, and artists closely studied the statue of Djoser walled up in a chapel against one side of the massive structure, seeking inspiration for how to represent some of Egypt's last indigenous kings.[12] A pyramid did not need to be 'true' to matter, in other words.

The straight-sided pyramid shape did seem to hold a particular significance in the Old Kingdom, for it represented rays of light emanating from the sun at a time when sun worship became an especially prominent feature of Egyptian religion. Kings of the 4th Dynasty were the first to be called 'the son of Re', the sun-god, in addition to 'the Horus', as earlier kings like Djoser were known. Horus and Re were both gods associated with falcons, but they had a different mythology and lineage, and perhaps originated in

Nineteenth-century photograph of the Step Pyramid at Saqqara, Egypt, *c.* 2650 BC.

different parts of the country. Horus was the avenging son of the mythical god-king Osiris, who had been murdered by his brother Seth, while Re was the embodiment of the sun itself. In later mythology Re would become a counterpart of Osiris, the former dominating the heavens, the latter the earth where the dead were buried. There is little hint of this mythology in the Old Kingdom, however; all we can say with confidence is that kings of this period paid increasing attention to monumentalizing the solar cult and emphasizing their own close relationship with the gods.

Building a pyramid took manpower, a strong communal identity and an efficient bureaucracy. As a result, only kings with stable reigns were likely to attempt it, and at times when the state was less centralized – the 'Intermediate Periods' in ancient Egyptian chronology – royal ambition set its sights lower. During the 12th and 13th dynasties of the Middle Kingdom, however, kings once again turned to the pyramid for their burial complexes. At sites around the Fayum, where some of these rulers were remembered for centuries afterwards, pyramids and sculpture-filled temples for the royal mortuary cult echoed the features and forms of earlier, Old Kingdom monuments.[13] Such studied repetition remained a feature of Egyptian art and architecture, since evoking the past in this self-conscious way reinforced a sense of unbroken authority and cultural continuity in the memory of the Egyptian people.

One reason for the Middle Kingdom's prosperity was the increasingly interconnected Mediterranean world of the Middle Bronze Age. Egypt benefited from trade and migration in every direction, a phenomenon that led to the formation of a competing power base in the Delta, where a series of rulers with non-Egyptian names – they seem to have originated in the western Levant – stepped in to fill a power vacuum at the end of the Middle Kingdom. Later histories remembered the reign of these Hyksos rulers (from the Egyptian for 'foreign kings') as a terrible upheaval; Manetho described it as a time when the gods punished Egypt. Societies collectively remember ruptures in their social fabric, as well as past glories, and the theme of a 'foreign' threat overcome by 'native' heroism resonated throughout Egyptian history – and with modern history writers, too.

Facts and fictions are difficult to untangle for this Second Intermediate Period, but leaders from the south of the country gained the upper hand through a series of battles. Around 1500 BC one of the southern leaders, a man named Ahmose from the town of Thebes (known today as Luxor), dealt a final defeat to the Hyksos rulers in the north and reunited the Delta and the Valley. This marked the start of the New Kingdom: the era most familiar to us today, thanks to famous rulers like Hatshepsut, Akhenaten, Tutankhamun and Ramses II 'the Great', and the fortuitous survival of their tombs and temples. Instead of pyramids, kings of this era secreted their burials underground in the Valley of the Kings, but the pyramid remained a meaningful form in Egyptian art and architecture. The tops of obelisks – tall, slender monoliths carved by royal order – preserved the familiar pyramid.[14] Throughout the New Kingdom rulers erected pairs of obelisks outside temple gateways. These were engineering feats: hewn from a single piece of stone, obelisks might be 30 to 40 metres long and weigh hundreds of tons. Most were made of red granite from the southern quarries at Aswan, so they had to be sailed down the Nile then erected on site: a potent visual manifestation not only of royal power, but of divine power as well. On a smaller scale, some non-royal individuals adopted the pyramid as a tomb marker, building metre-high mini-pyramids with sides that sloped at a steeper angle than the more familiar, squat pyramid shape atop obelisks, or at Giza. Single blocks of stone carved into a pyramid shape (often known as pyramidions in Egyptology) also served a devotional purpose, inscribed by priests and officials to record their prayers to the gods. In the 19th Dynasty a scribe named Ramose, who helped oversee work on tombs in the Valley of the Kings, had a pyramidion carved with images of himself on two sides and of two falcon gods (including Re-Horakhty, god of the evening horizon) on the others. Use of the pyramid form in a non-royal context appears to have become an acceptable way for men like Ramose to participate in the flourishing solar religion of the period.

As we saw above, after the end of the New Kingdom around 1000 BC, a weaker central state marked the Third and final 'Intermediate Period' of ancient Egyptian history. At times rival kings

A limestone 'pyramidion' from the top of the tomb of Ramose, a scribe, at Deir el-Medina, Egypt, *c.* 1250 BC.

governed the north and south of the country, and the powerful High Priests of Amun, the god of Thebes (Luxor), established their own family line as royal rulers, numbered the 21st Dynasty. Manetho's 25th Dynasty, composed of kings from Kush in modern Sudan, straddles the Third Intermediate Period and the ensuing Late Period.[15] The kingdom of Kush had a long history of its own and extensive links with Egypt through trade, migration and cultural exchange. The kings of Kush annexed Egypt around 750 BC after defeating the Assyrian forces that had been making inroads from the north. The Kushite kings already used Egyptian-inspired art and architecture for their own performances of power in Sudan, where their burials were marked by steep-sided pyramids at Nuri and el-Kurru, just below (that is, north of) the fourth cataract of the Nile, near the ancient city of Napata. Although some of the pyramids are only around 10 metres high, the largest are up to 30 metres, and the number of pyramids clustered together over time – several dozen for kings and queens at Nuri – make these cemeteries an impressive site. Numbered as the 25th Dynasty, five kings from Napata ruled Egypt for a century, before a fresh incursion from Assyria installed a new dynasty of Egyptian rulers and pushed the last king, Tantamani, back to Sudanese lands. But the pyramid remained a symbol of royal power in Sudan for centuries, reminding us that no single society or geographic location has a monopoly on cultural forms. Several centuries later, from around 300 BC to the fourth century AD, the centre of power in this region shifted further south to the city of Meroë, where it flourished as a gateway to trade with central, southern and eastern Africa. The kingdom of Meroë appears in several histories by Greek and Latin authors, who credit it with resisting attacks from Alexander the Great (which never happened) and the Roman Empire (which did). Its wealthy rulers could have been buried in any style they chose – and again they chose pyramids, rising from square bases at a 70-degree angle, with chapels built against one side.

Three thousand years separate the Step Pyramid of king Djoser and the last pyramid at Meroë, demonstrating not only the long time span of history in the Nile Valley, but the diversity of forms, influences and meanings that go into making any symbol, and any society, work. The pyramid form made the leap to Rome when the politician Gaius Cestius – influenced by Rome's recent conquest of Egypt – commissioned a Meroitic-like pyramid as his tomb around 15 BC.[16] It stands 36 metres high and was one of several pyramid-shaped monuments created around the same time. Such steep-sided pyramids became the norm in Western representations of all pyramids until the Napoleonic expedition. Thought to have associations with Freemasonry, the symbol of an all-knowing eye at the top of a pyramid has been the reverse of the Great Seal of the United States since 1782, and has appeared on the back of one-dollar bills since the 1930s. Thirteen courses of stone in the American pyramid represent the thirteen original states, while Latin mottoes emphasize divine approval for the new country. More than anything, the pyramid stands for the strength and durability the United States hoped to achieve – the same strength Napoleon hoped would inspire his troops, or shame them should they fail to meet his empire-building ambitions.

Alexander, the first Napoleon

Throughout this book, the transformation of ancient Egyptian civilization into different, sometimes competing, cultural memories is as important as timelines or maps. The pyramid has been a useful way to trace changes through the ancient history of Egypt, much as the figure of Thoth, in Chapter One, let us trace changes from Egypt's late antique history to the present day. Not only were forms of art and architecture, or gods and myths, vehicles for transmitting ideas about ancient Egypt to other cultures. So too were historical figures from the past, whose sometimes hazy biographies, or own self-mythologizing, made them ripe for later eras to reinterpret.

Having started this chapter with Napoleon's invasion of Egypt in 1798, we end it with Napoleon as well – and with the ancient hero he took as his model, Alexander the Great. Left to their own devices, the savants who accompanied the expedition set out to study the flora and fauna, geological resources, and art, crafts and architecture they had been tasked with recording. Under the leadership of Denon – later head of the Louvre and supporter of Gros – mapping, measuring and drawing ancient monuments and artefacts became a crucial part of their mission. Even though French troops had to surrender to the British all the antiquities they had collected, before returning home in defeat, the savants were allowed to keep their copious notes and drawings. Once back in Paris, they undertook a vast engraving and publishing project that culminated in more than twenty volumes published as the *Description de l'Égypte*, which appeared in stages between 1809 and 1829. Divided into three parts (modern state, natural history and antiquities), the *Description* made the results of the French expedition available to anyone with access to a learned library, or with the considerable financial resource to purchase a set, perhaps complete with a custom-made cabinet in an Egyptian-themed style. Yet the *Description* did something else as well: it imagined a modern and an ancient geography of Egypt ordered by European principles, analysed by European methods and subject to European control, which increasingly became a reality as the country's governor, Mohamed Ali, invited closer economic involvement.

In his own abortive quest for an empire in the Middle East, Napoleon could readily tap into the theme of the all-conquering

The recto (back) of the Great Seal of the United States of America, adopted in 1782 after a design by William Barton.

Frontispiece to the first volume of the *Description de l'Égypte* (1809).

Greek – that is, European – hero, Alexander the Great. At the beginning of his exhaustive campaign against the Persian Empire, Alexander led his troops into Egypt against little resistance. The Egyptian population seemed happy to lose their Persian overlords; and priests at the ancient city of Memphis, near the Giza pyramids, crowned him as a new pharaoh. For the frontispiece to the first volume of the *Description*, designers used the iconography of Alexander to praise Napoleon. Rather than represent Napoleon directly – only his monogram appears, topped by an imperial crown in the bottom page border – the artists depicted a heroically nude soldier urging on his chariot, at the top of the page. The names of French battle victories line each side of the border; behind the chariot, the Muses of ancient Greece symbolize the return of the arts to Egypt, or specifically – since they are next to Pompey's Pillar – Alexandria. The centre of the frontispiece is a Nilotic flight of fancy, gathering statues, sphinxes, obelisks and a classical column (Pompey's Pillar) in the foreground, while other temples and obelisks snake away up the river to the distant desert hills. Although it relates to geographic reality in that the foreground represents northern sites (like Giza) and the background the southern reaches of the Nile (Karnak on the left, Medinet Habu on the right, Philae in the distance), this is a landscape that feels like a pastiche and is empty of human presence, making it all the easier for Western viewers to place themselves within it or project their own ideas onto the scene. To the right, just behind Pompey's Pillar, the edge of a pyramid seems to hide in its own shadow – as if it knew what was coming and would rather have been someplace else.

THREE

SACRED SIGNS

Like many people who have visited Egypt, I own a souvenir necklace with my name spelled out in hieroglyphs on a pendant shaped like a cartouche, as the knotted rope ring that surrounds royal names is known. I confess that I have only worn it a few times, and never wore it again after someone I had never met before addressed me by my first name in a public place. I had forgotten that I was wearing the necklace, announcing my identity to anyone who could read a few Egyptian hieroglyphs – which is more people than you might expect. How different from the situation two centuries ago, when the most basic understanding of hieroglyphic signs had been lost for several centuries.

The cartouche emblazoned with my name used symbols that corresponded, one by one, to a single sound value, or phoneme: k, r, i, s, t, i, n, a. Since my name derives from Greek, there is no ancient Egyptian equivalent; it is a foreign word that can only be spelled out sound by sound. The same principle applied to the two cartouches that would help Thomas Young and Jean-François Champollion work out how to read Egyptian hieroglyphs in the early nineteenth century, by identifying familiar Greek names – Ptolemy and Cleopatra, king and queen of Egypt just after 200 BC – that were spelled out the same phonetic way in cartouches: p, t, o, l, m, i, s and k, l, i, o, p, t (or d), r, a. This was a revelation, because all the birds, body parts, geometric shapes and squiggled loops and lines used as Egyptian hieroglyphs had long been assumed to bear purely symbolic or philosophical meanings, rather than representing something so straightforward as a sound. Steeped in the ideas of the European Enlightenment, with its roots in the Renaissance, scholars reasoned that if they could decipher hieroglyphic writing, the lost wisdom of ancient Egypt and Hermes Trismegistus would be restored to them, repairing the memory loss that the historical divide between Islamic Egypt and Christian Europe had created.

Lost wisdom, mysterious symbols: quite a lot was riding on being able to read the copious inscriptions with which ancient Egyptian sculptors had covered temples, obelisks and statues, or that scribes had inked in black and red on the surfaces of papyrus scrolls. Among the Egyptian antiquities the British army seized from French troops at their 1801 surrender was the chunk of dark grey stone bearing the names of Ptolemy and Cleopatra that proved pivotal for both Young and Champollion. On one face, the stone bore tightly packed rows of inscription in three scripts and two languages: Egyptian written in the Demotic script, Egyptian hieroglyphs and Greek. Its significance had been obvious to the French officer who oversaw its removal from a defensive wall at el-Rashid in the western Nile Delta, better known in European languages as Rosetta.[1]

This chapter explores how hieroglyphs and other writing systems functioned in ancient Egypt, and how (or whether) the ancient language was ever 'lost'. We start at the beginning, with the invention – for that is what it was – of the hieroglyphic writing system in the Protodynastic period when a centralized state headed by a king first emerged in the Nile Valley. Several languages and writing systems were used in ancient Egypt, and understanding literacy rates and the social uses of writing is important for understanding how language use evolved during the Ptolemaic, Roman and Byzantine eras. In the medieval Arab world, Egyptian hieroglyphs were just as fascinating to many scholars as they would prove to be in early modern Europe. Islamic scholarship on hieroglyphic writing has been little known in the West, however, even though it was one source used by the seventeenth-century Jesuit scholar Athanasius Kircher in his own studies of Egyptian inscriptions. Kircher's mystical interpretations emphasized the sacred and symbolic character of the signs, and it was only the much later insights of Young and Champollion, both of whom had studied many ancient and modern languages, that convinced European scholars of the Egyptian language's more mundane aspects. Like every language, ancient Egyptian had grammar, syntax and vocabulary. It just expressed these in a writing system that depicted animals and everyday objects, instead of using more abstract characters or cuneiform wedges. In the past 150 years Egyptology has systemized an approach to reading, recording and analysing ancient Egyptian texts. Many of these do concern the mysteries of the universe, or something along those lines, but just as many are government edicts, adventure stories and mortgages. The concerns of ancient Egyptian society became a little more clear – but as it turns out, no less complex.

In the beginning was the hieroglyph

Any mention of the Rosetta Stone invites talk of keys, codes and decipherment, as if we still suspect that the ancient Egyptians were hiding secrets from would-be readers. There is, in fact, something to that. Today, living in societies with near-total literacy, we assume that writing something down means that anyone can read it. But this is a relatively recent phenomenon, and by no means a universal one. In societies where few people can read, writing and, crucially, the display of writing can reinforce the authority held by ruling institutions, like the Christian Church in medieval Europe. Estimates suggest that only between 2 and 5 per cent of the population in ancient Egypt could read and write at any period, and not all of those individuals would have full command of the different scripts in use. Imagine yourself in a room full of 100 people, having to rely on just two or three of them to write an email, draw up a loan agreement or read out a government notice. Much would depend on trust.

The very word – hieroglyphs – that ancient Greek writers applied to Egyptian picture-writing had the literal meaning 'sacred carvings', and this itself offers a clue as to the use of the pictorial writing system familiar to us today, with all its birds and body parts. Hieroglyphic writing did have a sacred character, in that the ancient Egyptians used it almost exclusively in contexts evoking the divine world: on coffins and statues, in tombs and temples, or on high-status jewellery, furniture and weaponry like that found in the tomb of Tutankhamun. Hieroglyphs were formal, like the best italic calligraphy. They were also closely connected to the distinctive system of representation used in Egyptian art, which suggests that hieroglyphic writing developed at the same time as methods for drawing and carving other kinds of images. Writing and art go together in ancient Egypt: both favour profiles for clarity in representing faces and limbs; both scale objects up or down to show relationships of status, or to help signs fit together; and both obey rules of orientation, so that all signs and images face in the same direction. Having all the signs facing the viewer's right (most obvious for human and animal figures) was the dominant orientation, and since Egyptian is conventionally written from right to left, like Arabic and Hebrew, the reader 'faces' the human and animal signs. But hieroglyphs could also be reversed, reading left to right, where a decorative scheme required it, for instance to create a symmetrical composition or to make both walls of a tomb 'face' an offering placed at the far end. The same held true for other two-dimensional images, although statues, and other three-dimensional figures, always represented men (rarely, women) with the left leg advanced, regardless of where the statue would be placed or how the object would be used.

Hieroglyphic writing appears around 3200 BC in the late Pre-dynastic or Protodynastic period, at the same time as a sudden and significant change in art. It is probably not too strong to speak of these new visual forms as having been invented to suit the needs of the rulers of the new Egyptian state. The decorated pottery, small stone palettes for grinding cosmetic paint, and slender, almost cylindrical, free-standing sculpture of preceding centuries gave way to novel or scaled-up object forms that could exploit the potential of the new pictorial representation in full. On an over-sized, double-sided cosmetic palette depicting king Narmer, images of the king and his entourage obey the core principles that Egyptian art would adopt for more than 3,000 years. Likewise groups of hieroglyphic signs are readily legible, like the name of the king ('fierce catfish') at the top of the palette, inside a square, patterned frame representing the royal residence. Writing went hand in hand with the creation of a centralized state because it filled a bureaucratic need for keeping records of transactions and for labelling raw materials and processed goods. At the same time, their decorative value and restricted use also made hieroglyphs well suited to the ceremony and symbolism of Egyptian kingship.

Most hieroglyphic signs have a phonetic value, that is, they represent a sound produced in speech. Some signs, like those used to spell my name, or Cleopatra's, in a cartouche, represent a single sound, others two or three sounds together. In addition to the hieroglyphs that write the sounds of a word, other hieroglyphs may indicate gender (male/female), number (singular or plural) and the specific sense in which the word is being used.[2] This last sign, which Egyptologists call a determinative, appears at the end of a word and helps clarify its meaning, where two or three similar meanings might be possible, or classify the qualities of the idea being expressed. The determinative of a sparrow, for instance, classified words that had negative associations, or signalled smallness, while the determinative of two human legs indicated anything to do with motion. Not every hieroglyph was pronounced (determinatives never were), and not everything that was pronounced had a hieroglyphic sign. True vowel sounds were not written down, probably because these sounds changed when the tense or number of the word changed. The reader would know what vowel sounds were needed, so that writing only consonants (or near-consonants, like 'o' and 'y' sounds) made perfect sense. Modern Arabic and Hebrew work in a similar way, often omitting vowels in written form. Ancient Egyptian belongs to the language family known as Afroasiatic or Hamito-Semitic. Although it has many distinctive features, it also has a number of similarities both with Semitic languages, such as Hebrew, Arabic and ancient Akkadian, and with North African ('Hamitic') languages, such as Hausa (spoken in Niger and Nigeria) and Berber (spoken across the Sahara).

Hieroglyphs were only one of the writing systems used in ancient Egypt. When scribes wrote on sheets of papyrus, using ink and a reed brush, the action suited a more flowing form of script. Reducing the hieroglyphic signs to outline forms that could be written more smoothly and rapidly yielded a script the Greeks called hieratic, meaning 'priestly', although in fact hieratic had much wider and more commonplace use. Hieratic could be written in a decorative style suited to prestige documents like wills or *Book of the Dead* papyri, but it tended to serve more run-of-the-mill purposes, for instance in contracts, letters and receipts. Hieratic script was the engine of Egyptian society for much of its ancient history, the everyday writing that village scribes or temple copyists deployed for legal and administrative purposes, or to make new versions of library scrolls that were wearing out. Boys training to be scribes, who were taught to read and write in schools attached to their local temples, would have learned hieratic first, not the more specialized hieroglyphic script that students of ancient Egyptian start with today.

Languages change quickly as they are spoken, but writing systems tend to lag behind, replicating a more staid form of the language that suited certain contexts precisely because of its age and authority, rather like the early seventeenth-century phrases of the King James Bible that resonate when recited in some church services today. The hieratic script was better than hieroglyphic writing at keeping up with language change. Egyptologists divide major shifts in the grammar and vocabulary of ancient Egyptian into Old Egyptian, Middle Egyptian and Late Egyptian, although unlike the similarly named time periods of Egyptian history, these stages do not always follow each other in sequence. Middle Egyptian was used for hieroglyphic inscriptions, especially in temples, as late as the Ptolemaic period, while Late Egyptian, which was roughly the language king Tutankhamun spoke around 1325 BC, survives chiefly in hieratic. From around 650 BC a stage of ancient Egyptian known as Demotic came to be written down in its own script, an even more reductive form than hieratic. This is the script that appears in the middle of the Rosetta Stone, where it is more fully preserved than either the hieroglyphic or Greek texts. The Demotic form of Egyptian was only ever written in Demotic script, and vice versa. Surviving Demotic texts include everything from marriage contracts to abstruse religious discussions: thousands of papyri still await translation, since few scholars specialize in Demotic today.

Demotic flourished at a time when Greek had become the main language of the state, yet it is almost entirely free of vocabulary borrowed from Greek, as if Egyptian priests and scribes, who were responsible for composing and writing down Demotic texts, had made a conscious choice to exclude foreign words. Instead, the form of Egyptian spoken in Ptolemaic and Roman times is what we know as Coptic, which continues to be used as the language of the Coptic Christian church liturgy in Egypt. The Coptic script appeared in the first century AD, using the Greek alphabet of 24 letters plus an additional eight letters for Egyptian sounds not represented in Greek. Coptic thus could write some of the vowel sounds and shifts that scripts derived from hieroglyphs did not; it also lacked the other scripts' links to Egyptian religion, which became an important consideration as more people converted to Christianity in the Roman and Byzantine eras. In contrast to Demotic, Coptic owes a substantial part of its vocabulary to Greek, perhaps as much as 40 per cent. Both languages were spoken in Egypt until around the sixth century. After the expansion of Islam and Arabic-speaking culture into Egypt in the seventh century, Arabic and Coptic coexisted for centuries, although each gradually (though not exclusively) became associated with the Islamic and Christian religions many of their speakers practised. Language diversity was always present in Egypt, as it is in many societies today. Bilingualism or multilingualism, and using different languages for different purposes, would have been a feature of life for many people in ancient Egypt, long before the changes introduced by Hellenistic Greek rule. In the New Kingdom, for instance, Akkadian was the language of international diplomacy, as we know from discoveries of cuneiform tablets sent between Egypt and Iraq. Minority languages and regional dialects have not survived in written form, however, making ancient Egypt appear to be a more homogeneous society than it actually was. Writing conferred power, and it was the power of hieroglyphic writing in particular that tantalized, especially as it fell ever further out of use.

Secrets and signs

A census taken in the early second century AD, in the provincial capital Oxyrhynchus ('Sharp-nosed fish'), records that there were two hieroglyph-cutters active in the town.[3] One wonders how they kept themselves occupied, but perhaps there was enough work to be had completing or repairing inscriptions in the Egyptian-style temples that still operated, or fulfilling the occasional new commission for a stela or a statue. Carving hieroglyphic inscriptions was a dying art in Roman Egypt, almost a heritage industry. By the late second century AD it was rare to see coherent hieroglyphic inscriptions, although some still appear painted on intentionally old-fashioned-looking coffins and burial shrouds.[4] Over the next hundred years or so, knowledge of how to read and write hieroglyphs gradually dwindled to a few ageing specialists, likewise the Demotic and hieratic scripts, which ceased to be employed as Coptic gained acceptance. But interactions between languages and choices of script depended on an individual's or social group's priorities, making it impossible to pinpoint when knowledge of a language, or its written form, died out. In early third-century Thebes, for instance, papyrus handbooks of Egyptian prayers, rituals and magical invocations were written down in Demotic but have marginal notes in both Old Coptic and Greek, because the people compiling and using these scrolls were comfortable translating religious formulae across all three language forms.[5] Egyptologists can identify the last securely dated hieroglyphic inscription, carved in AD 394, in the temple of Isis at Philae, in the far south of Egypt; the temple also has the latest Demotic inscription, from AD 452. That there was any effort at keeping the old scripts and languages alive shows how important they were to the self-identity of Egyptian culture, and how different languages and religious beliefs coexist.

Sometime in the fifth century an Egyptian priest or scholar named Horapollo saw a need for a study of Egyptian hieroglyphs that would expound the pictorial writing system to audiences literate in Greek. Accounts differ as to who exactly Horapollo was, where he lived (perhaps Alexandria) and whether he is in fact the author of the most famous work ascribed to him, the *Hieroglyphica*.[6] A manuscript of the *Hieroglyphica* discovered on the Greek island of Andros was acquired by a Florentine nobleman travelling in Greece in the early fifteenth century. He brought it back to Florence, where it caused a stir in humanist circles of the Italian Renaissance, especially after the leading Venetian printer Aldus Manutius published an edition in 1505. A Latin translation followed a few years later, bringing the text into wider circulation. The *Hieroglyphica* sets out to interpret 189 hieroglyphic signs, which it does chiefly through allegorical readings of what they represent. To Renaissance scholars eager to supplement their knowledge of ancient Egypt, alongside their studies of ancient Greece and Rome, Horapollo's work was a godsend. Giordano Bruno and Erasmus were just two of many who drew inspiration from it.

Unfortunately, Horapollo had no idea what he was talking about. Or rather, he had *an* idea, but it bears little relationship to what we now understand about the phonetic and ideographic values of Egyptian hieroglyphs. Instead, the associations he drew between signs and their meanings must reflect ideas that had already developed, presumably among Egyptian specialists themselves, about the metaphorical and magical significance of hieroglyphic writing. Many of the interpretations proposed in the text derive from extrapolations about the object or, especially, animal that a sign represents. For the hieroglyph of a swallow, which was used to write the word *wer*, 'great', Horapollo offers the meaning 'inheritance from parents to their sons', because the female swallow (he asserts) rolls herself in mud to build a nest for her young when she herself is about to die. Other interpretations in the *Hieroglyphica* do capture the essence of the ancient Egyptian sign, even if Horapollo augments or explains it with associations we do not recognize today. The jackal hieroglyph, for instance, he identifies with embalmers, one link it had in ancient Egypt thanks to the jackal-headed god Anubis, who mummified the dead. But Horapollo broadens the meaning of the jackal (or dog) sign to include scribes and the spleen, among other things. Each suggested meaning has an explanation in the animal itself: scribes because,

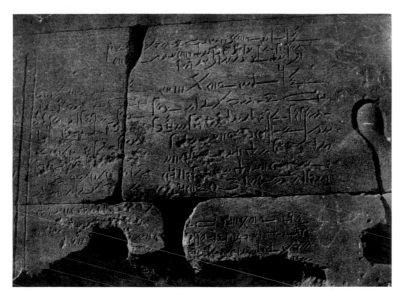

Maxime Du Camp, photograph taken between 1849 and 1851 of a Demotic inscription at the temple of Isis, Philae, dating to the 4th century AD. Salted paper print, 1852.

like dogs, they are fierce and protective, and the spleen because in the jackal or dog this organ was considered weak, according to medical principles of the time.

Even if we dismiss the *Hieroglyphica* as an accurate or useful guide to hieroglyphs, it both reflects, and helped shape, ideas about emblems and symbolic expression that were current among the intelligentsia of sixteenth- and seventeenth-century Europe. It also appeared to confirm what other Greek and Latin texts had to say about the astonishing knowledge and secret wisdom possessed by the Egyptians. Scholars in Europe hoped that Horapollo would help them translate the few inscriptions that were available at that time, especially in Italy where hieroglyphic inscriptions could be found on Egyptian antiquities imported in Roman times – or ancient Roman versions of Egyptian monuments, not that early modern viewers could tell the difference. The narrow selection of signs Horapollo discussed, however, and the circumlocutory way in which he discussed them offered little practical guidance.

In Egypt, Arab scholars faced a similar dilemma. There was ample interest throughout the medieval period in the picture writing of ancient Egyptian culture, given that hieroglyphs covered temples, tombs, and the statues and other objects that were regularly unearthed or reused, up and down the country. Because Coptic and Arabic coexisted for several centuries in Egypt, some scholars in the medieval Arab world had a better understanding of Egyptian scripts than Horapollo and his Renaissance admirers. Ibn Wahshiyah, who lived in the ninth century, was one of the best known of these scholars, whose work was copied and circulated for centuries; he recognized that some hieroglyphs were phonetic, while others represented ideas.[7] Arab writers like Ibn Wahshiyah were themselves familiar with Horapollo, and among alchemists and Sufi mystics (the two often went together) the symbolic aspects of hieroglyphic writing held a strong appeal, as did the decorative potential, proportions and symmetry of all the ancient Egyptian scripts. Arabic calligraphy, especially as practised in medieval Sufism, shared similar aesthetic values, while alchemy, which was an important branch of science in the medieval Arab world, appreciated the cryptographic use of hieroglyphic signs, which ancient Egyptian priests had developed into an art form in some temples and papyri. Writing that offered the potential for double meanings and concealment could be translated into something better than words: power.

Fountains of fantasy

The Mediterranean connected Christian Europe and the Islamic Middle East, even at times when political divisions or military conflicts, like the Crusades, disrupted diplomatic relations and trade between the different powers. People moved, and where people moved, objects moved – like the manuscript of Horapollo first brought to Florence from Ottoman Greece in the fifteenth century. Because of these exchanges, and the active seeking out of ancient manuscripts for early modern collectors in Europe, the work of Arab scholars was as readily available to learned men as that of Greek and Latin authors, as long as one mastered the necessary languages. One man who did – he knew more than a dozen languages, including Arabic, Coptic, Hebrew and Syriac – was Father Athanasius Kircher (1601/2–1680), a German-born

Jesuit priest who spent the latter part of his career teaching and researching in the order's college in Rome.[8] Kircher was a man of letters in the Baroque fashion, a polymath with interests not only in languages, ancient Egypt and China, but in hydraulics, mathematics and volcanology. He enjoyed the patronage of the Habsburg Holy Roman emperors and, in Rome, popes Urban VIII, Innocent X and Alexander VII. Although interest in Kircher's work has grown in academic circles over the past twenty or thirty years, by the end of his own lifetime younger thinkers were already treating his vast output with some scepticism, and Kircher found no favour with Enlightenment-influenced scholars like Jean-François Champollion, who would decipher Egyptian hieroglyphs in the 1820s.

Kircher flourished at a specific juncture in European science and the history of ideas. The Renaissance rediscovery of ancient Greek and Latin texts, like Horapollo's *Hieroglyphica*, went hand in hand with the study of texts in the so-called Oriental languages like Hebrew and Arabic, because the entire Mediterranean and Middle Eastern world appeared to European eyes as part of European heritage. From Athens to Alexandria, from Jerusalem to Babylon in Iraq, from Turkish Anatolia to Palmyra and Persia: in the sixteenth and seventeenth centuries these multicultural, multilingual geographic reaches were all considered to have played a role in the formation of Christian culture. As the Protestant Reformation and, in Kircher's youth, the Catholic Counter-Reformation rocked Europe, understanding this heritage took on new urgency. That is one reason why sixteenth- and seventeenth-century scholars treated the philosophy attributed to Hermes Trismegistus as seriously as the philosophy of Aristotle or Plato, even more so. Ideas that now seem esoteric comfortably coexisted with Christian theology. Parsing hieroglyphic inscriptions for the lost wisdom of the ancient Egyptians presented no problem for a Catholic priest like Kircher, or the popes he served.

When Pope Innocent X, from Rome's powerful Pamphili family, commissioned a fountain to stand in front of his ancestral palace in the Piazza Navona, he turned to two men for the design: Rome's leading sculptor, Gian Lorenzo Bernini, and its leading scholar,

Kircher.[9] The fountain symbolized the supremacy and global reach of the Catholic Church, from the rocky terrain at the bottom referencing its founder, St Peter, to the four famous river sculptures representing Africa (the Nile), Europe (the Danube), Asia (the Ganges) and South America (the Río de la Plata). Rising up from the rivers was a 16.5-metre high, red granite obelisk carved with Egyptian hieroglyphs and topped with the Pamphili family dove. This particular obelisk had been quarried in Aswan, southern Egypt, in the first century AD on behalf of emperor Domitian. It probably stood in front of temples dedicated to the Egyptian goddess Isis and her Hellenistic consort Serapis near the centre of Rome, and its hieroglyphic inscriptions, perhaps composed by Egyptian priests resident in the city, include Domitian's full name and the title *autocrator* (emperor), transcribed phonetically. In AD 309 emperor Maxentius moved the obelisk to the new Circus he had built, where it probably toppled over, or was felled, during the unrest of the seventh century. By the time Bernini re-erected it in 1649, it had lain in five pieces for centuries.

Creating the fountain and repairing the obelisk were expensive undertakings in straitened economic times, which did not stop Innocent X raising taxes on Rome's urban poor to pay for it all.[10] Kircher obliged by making a complete study of the obelisk, which he published as an illustrated book in 1650, including his translation (as he saw it) of the Egyptian inscriptions. Confident in his command of hieroglyphs, he also advised Bernini's workshop on how to fill the gaps in the ancient inscription where the obelisk had been broken, as a result of which the hieroglyphs, already composed in a distinctive, Roman-period style, look especially odd today.

The great Kircher was not infallible: he was once forced to concede that the hieroglyphs on another obelisk he had 'translated' were the work of an artist's imagination.[11] It was an embarrassing episode. Influential and well connected as he was, other scholars were sceptical of Kircher's work during his own lifetime, and his elaborately printed books fell from favour after his death. In retrospect, Kircher seems like a link between the 'lost' knowledge of reading hieroglyphs and the triumphant moment in 1822 when

Gian Lorenzo Bernini, *Four Rivers Fountain*, Piazza Navona, Rome, 1648–51, supporting an obelisk from the reign of emperor Domitian, late 1st century AD.

Champollion announced his decipherment of the script. But this assumes that knowledge emerges in a linear line of progression, whereby the accurate study of evidence leads us ever closer to some truth. The changing fashion for Kircher's ideas demonstrates that knowledge does not work that way: what we know, or think we know, is created and recreated at different times, in different circumstances. Moreover, knowledge is never free from the concerns of politics, religion and other influences; witness the way the Arabic sources Kircher used have since been downplayed, distancing the contributions of Middle Eastern scholars. Accuracy and evidence are just as changeable, since opinions have varied over time about what constitutes evidence and how best to identify and interpret it. Today, academics consider the changing valuation of evidence and argument to be essential to the study of knowledge, known as epistemology.

In eighteenth-century Europe the Enlightenment reacted against previous modes of thought like Kircher's, divorcing 'religion' and 'science' and establishing the modes of academic discourse more familiar to us now. A new standard of evidence-based inquiry called for direct study, the use of measuring and recording devices, and, increasingly, the professionalization of scholarship in institutes, museums and universities. Hence the rationale for Napoleon's scientific expedition, in which savants and soldiers alike hunted for ancient manuscripts and monuments alongside their map-making, mineral-sourcing and military strategizing. Had Athanasius Kircher known about the Rosetta Stone, would he have parsed the Demotic and hieroglyphs in relation to the Greek text, or would he have dealt with it in much the same way as he had the Piazza Navona obelisk, interpreting them as metaphorical expressions independent of legible and logical Greek? Some 150 years later, perhaps it was not so much that Champollion was the right man for the Rosetta Stone, but that the Stone had appeared at the right time.

Acts of translation

How the Rosetta Stone came to be in the British Museum is written directly on it, in a fourth language that few viewers seem to notice: English. On the hewn sides of the Stone, white-painted lettering reads, on one side, 'Captured in Egypt by the British Army in 1801', and on the other, 'Presented by King George III'. The massive stone – it measures 112 cm long, 76 cm wide and 28 cm thick – was uncovered by the French army during operations at Fort St Julien at Rosetta (el-Rashid) in the Delta in July 1799.

The lieutenant in charge, Pierre-François Bouchard, recognized its potential importance and brought it to the attention of division commander General Jacques-François Menou, who was governor of the province under the French occupation – and who, coincidentally, later converted to Islam, took the name Abdullah and married an Egyptian woman. Menou ensured that the discovery of the Stone, with its three distinct scripts, was announced to the Institut d'Égypte, which Napoleon had established in Cairo as the home of the savants. Copies were made by inking the stone and using it as a printing plate, with the results sent back to France in hopes that scholars there could make some headway with the hieroglyphic script at the top.[12]

In 1800 Menou became head of the French army in Egypt following the assassination of Napoleon's right-hand man, General Kléber, who had been trying to reach a truce with the British. Instead, it fell to Menou to try to shore up French military efforts in Egypt. After a prolonged siege at Alexandria, Menou surrendered to the British in 1801. In negotiating the terms of the surrender, Menou preserved the scientific expedition's notes, maps and drawings, arguing that they were private property and thus not subject to martial laws. He tried the same argument to keep possession of a number of antiquities, but British officers insisted on treating moveable monuments as state (that is, French) property unless they could clearly be shown to be personal goods. Menou tried to keep the Rosetta Stone concealed among his own belongings, but British officers spotted it, deemed it unlikely to be merely for Menou's own use, and shipped the Stone to London in 1802 on the appropriately named captured French frigate, HMS *Egyptienne*. The Society of Antiquaries displayed the Stone at their rooms in Somerset House and had plaster casts of it made for the leading British universities of the day, as well as further print copies. Together with other monuments and statues seized from the French, the Rosetta Stone went on display in the British Museum in the summer of 1802.[13]

Visitors to the museum commented, often unfavourably, on the contrast between the dark colours and stiff contours of the Egyptian objects and the flowing white marble of the Classical sculptures displayed nearby. However, the chief interest in the Rosetta Stone was not what it looked like, but what it said. Its specialist terminology meant that even reading the Greek inscription took some effort. The French scholar Silvestre de Sacy (whom we met earlier in this chapter) recognized the middle script as Demotic, and in collaboration with the Swedish diplomat and linguist Johan Åkerblad managed to identify a few Greek names among the Demotic signs. It was de Sacy who remarked, in a letter to the British scientist Thomas Young, that comparing the royal names in Greek and Demotic to the cartouche-encircled signs in the hieroglyphic script might be a fruitful approach – and so it proved, for Young was able to work out the alphabetic spellings of names like Ptolemy, publishing his results in 1819.

In the meantime, Young also corresponded with de Sacy's younger rival in France, Jean-François Champollion. Champollion consulted not only prints of the Rosetta Stone, but copies of other inscriptions circulating at the time, in particular a bilingual Greek and Egyptian obelisk owned by explorer William John Bankes (who first recorded it at the temple of Isis on Philae in 1815, and in the 1820s had it transported to Kingston Lacy, his country

Scholars attending the International Congress of Orientalists examine the Rosetta Stone in the British Museum, 1874.

home in Dorset). Helped by his knowledge of Coptic and the dual Greek–Egyptian inscriptions, Champollion finally produced a near-complete sign list of Egyptian hieroglyphs with their phonetic values, published in a letter to the French Academy in September 1822. He also recognized that hieroglyphic words included signs that were not pronounced, and it was this combination of insights that enabled him to translate hieroglyphic texts in a meaningful way. Champollion became a leading figure in the new field of Egyptology, although his early death at age 42, just ten years after he announced the decipherment, meant that he taught few students and published only a fraction of his work.

The ability to translate ancient Egyptian texts revealed how weird and wonderful they can be – and how normal, too. Anyone still expecting Hermes Trismegistus' guide to the mysteries of the universe was bound to be disappointed, as was anyone expecting the act of translation to be straightforward. The Rosetta Stone proved to be a case in point, with each of the three scripts conveying a similar, but not identical, version of a decree issued in 196 BC by the young king Ptolemy v. The Demotic text, which is the most complete, begins with a long list of the king's Egyptian names and expressions for the date, before recounting everything he had done to benefit Egyptian priests and their temples, including reductions in taxes and giving up his claims to certain temple revenues. In return, the priests agreed to install a statue of Ptolemy,

> together with a statue for the local god, giving him a scimitar of victory, in each temple, in the public part of the temple, they being made in the manner of Egyptian work; and the priests should pay service to the statues in each temple three times a day, and they should lay down sacred objects before them and do for them the rest of the things that it is normal to do, in accordance with what is done for the other gods on the festivals, the processions, and the named days.[14]

If this was done in every major temple, it represented a significant undertaking, especially since versions of the same decree, since discovered on other stela fragments, confirm that it applied throughout Egypt. Scholars today surmise that the capitulations indicate how much Ptolemy v needed the support of the indigenous priesthood at a time of civil strife.

With breaks at the top, bottom and sides, the Rosetta Stone is clearly a fragment of a larger monument – but what kind? Until 1999 the British Museum displayed the Rosetta Stone lying on its back at an angle, as if it were a book resting on a giant stand. This presentation of the Stone was in keeping with the way it had been treated ever since French troops identified it: as a text to be read in the way that contemporary readers hold books or papers. Applying ink to the surface to print copies emphasized its page-like character. The British Museum also applied a layer of wax to the Stone in the early nineteenth century, to try to protect it from the dirt and oil of human hands; the Stone was displayed uncovered, and visitors were eager to touch the famous object. By 1981 the surface of the Stone was so dark that the Museum added white paint to the incised writing in order to make the inscriptions stand out.

Conservation work undertaken for a special exhibition in 1999 was able to remove the accumulated layers and reveal the Stone's original appearance: a mottled grey granodiorite, with a streak of pink stone running through its broken upper edge. In addition, the Museum decided to display the Rosetta Stone in its original intended position, since it had been designed in antiquity to stand upright as a free-standing stela. Reconstructions based on similar monuments suggest that the Stone extended another 50 cm or so to a rounded top, which would have been carved with Egyptian-style images of Ptolemy before the gods of the temple in which the Stone stood. Although probably set up in a semi-public space, like a temple forecourt, the Stone was not intended as a text that people would stop to read. Even if they knew how to read any of the scripts, the terminology is so specialist, and the text inscribed so small and low down, that reading and understanding it would be a challenge. Instead, like the first hieroglyphs used in the earliest days of the Egyptian kings, the Rosetta Stone used writing to display knowledge and privilege. The Rosetta Stone was never an

An artist's reconstruction of what the Rosetta Stone looked like in antiquity.

open book, whether on plain view in a temple or in a museum. In the wake of Champollion's decipherment, European scholars thought they had finally unlocked the secrets of ancient Egypt, but at the risk of forgetting why secrets were written down in the first place.

FOUR

TAKEN IN THE FLOOD

The re-erected obelisk of Domitian in the Piazza Navona in Rome rises from a fountain designed by the masterful Baroque sculptor and architect, Bernini. One of the four river-themed sculptures that adorn the fountain is the Nile, shown as a bearded man perched on a cliff near a palm tree. With his raised left arm, he struggles to lift the cloth that covers his head and face. Only from a vantage point beneath the sculpture can viewers glimpse his flowing beard and the lower half of his veiled face. Representing the Nile as a mature, well-muscled man was a style inspired by ancient Roman statues of the river-god Nilus (in Greek, *Neilos*), while the cloth that conceals his face is a symbol of the Nile's source, which was then unknown to Europeans.

Ancient Greek and Roman writers were likewise intrigued by the source of the Nile and its annual flood. To them, it symbolized the ultimate mystery of the universe, an idea not far removed from the ancient Egyptians' own reverence for the Nile. One ancient Egyptian vision of the Nile's geography imagined caverns far to the south where the swelling flood waters gathered before bursting past the cataracts around Aswan and gradually filling the flood plain all the way to the Delta and the Mediterranean Sea. The south in general, and the Nile in particular, was thus the font of all creation. The flood started each year in July, when Sirius, the dog star – in ancient Egyptian, Sopdet (or Greek, *Sothis*) – reappeared on the dawn horizon. Since the flood deposited the rich silt in which Egyptian farmers planted their crops, the success of the next year's agricultural cycle depended on an adequate, but not excessive, flood. The waters were life, and their rhythmic recurrence offered a ready metaphor for creation and rebirth. The disappearance of Sopdet, and other stars, for seventy days before rising over the horizon again, helped define the seventy-day period of embalming and mummification for the dead.

Taking the Nile as its theme, this chapter looks at the importance of the river and the riverscape to ancient Egyptian thought, as well as the ways in which the Nile and its annual flood shaped other cultures' ideas about Egypt. The topic remains timely in light of ongoing disputes over water rights in northeast Africa, not to mention the impact the Aswan High Dam has had on agriculture and rural life in Egypt since it was constructed in the 1960s. Herodotus famously described Egypt as 'the gift of the Nile', and since the development of mass tourism in the nineteenth century, the river has inspired other travellers with its picturesque scenery and romantic associations. Over the centuries, however, the Nile riverscape has changed more substantially than tourists imagine. Grazing water buffalo, felucca sailboats and a shore lined with ruined temples may evoke a sense of timelessness, but even before twentieth-century damming projects put an end to the annual flood, human minds had imagined the river in several different ways, and human actions had measured its waters and managed its banks to suit the needs of many different regimes.

Water worlds

Rivers and floods were powerful themes in the dry ancient cultures of the Middle East, where settled agricultural communities first formed along waterways such as the Nile, the Tigris and the Euphrates. From the Babylonian and biblical accounts of a great flood that nearly destroyed the world, to Moses' magical control of the Red Sea, which drowned the army of pharaoh in the Book of Exodus, water represented moments of crisis – and opportunity. According to Exodus, Moses himself had gained a new, more prosperous start in life when his Hebrew mother placed him in a pitch-tarred basket and floated him on the Nile, where pharaoh's daughter found the baby and raised him as her own. 'Moses' is an ancient Egyptian name, most often used with the name of a god to mean that the person is 'born of' that god and under divine protection. The baby in the basket seemed to be born of the river itself.

Despite, or perhaps because of, its centrality to Egyptian life and thought, the Nile was not worshipped as a god per se, but the Nile in flood was referred to as Hapi, a divine figure who personified its life-giving character.[1] There were no temples dedicated to the Nile, and no cycles of myths that turned Hapi into a human protagonist, the way that stories were told about Osiris' sister-wife Isis and their son Horus; in fact, the goddess's tears for her dead husband were sometimes said to be the source of the flood. When Hapi himself is represented or named in hieroglyphs, the sign for 'water' (three wavy lines: ∿∿∿) often acts as the determinative at the end of his name, rather than the usual determinatives for gods and goddesses (another indication that although Egyptians associated the river and its flood waters with the sacred, they were too vast to be contained easily by a single deity). Images of Hapi did appear in the visual arts, however, sometimes on his own but more often as a pair or series of figures that used the same body form – a man with a generous belly, drooping chest, and blue or green skin colour – to represent the idea of a fertile natural world, well nourished by the flood-fed land. Egyptologists refer to these as 'fecundity figures'; they often carry trays of offerings, including jars of Nile water and stems of papyrus and water lily. Fecundity figures adorn the square sides of the thrones the Egyptian king sits on, and the lowest bands of decoration on temple and tomb walls. Through these figures, the Nile quite literally supports state and society in ancient Egypt.

Flowing downstream towards the Mediterranean basin, the Nile current made for easy sailing from south to north. A prevailing wind from the north also helped sailors navigate upriver, and from the earliest days of Egyptian history the Nile was the primary means of communication and transport. The river and its banks provided a habitat for many animals, including birds and fish (the latter being the main source of protein in the ancient diet). In the Delta, multiple tributaries created a marshy environment

Bronze plaque, perhaps from a shrine, showing the god of the Nile flood, Hapi, c. 600 BC.

that was the most productive agricultural region in Egypt. In the Nile Valley, flood plains on either side of the river received rich, silty soil in which farmers could plant two cycles of crop per year, such as flax for linen and wheat and vegetables for food. Natural pools and man-made basins or canals could help store river water for the dry season, or create better access by boat to important structures, like temples. The fulcrum-balanced *shaduf* (its Arabic name) could help lift water on a modest scale, but mechanized means of irrigation, such as the water wheel and the Archimedes screw, were only introduced much later, in Ptolemaic and Roman times.

The impact the Nile flood had on day-to-day life arguably encouraged cooperation and bureaucratic organization, since people living upriver would be able to tell weeks in advance of those downstream if the flood was going to be higher or lower than average. Poor floods threatened famine, while excessive floods would destroy settlements along the plains. This could not be controlled, except by divine will. At best, it could be managed by advance planning, for instance using measuring devices to judge the river level (known as Nilometers) and keeping meticulous records of past floods, to try to predict patterns or recall what precautions were taken. Commanding the chaos of the natural world was a recurring theme in Egyptian literature and art, and many of the artworks we admire today for their poise or charming details in fact betray an anxious concern with keeping nature in check. Carved into the limestone block walls of his tomb's offering chapel, the Dynasty 5 official Ti stands serenely on a small skiff made of bound papyrus stems, which itself rests on the zigzagged surface of the water – not the Nile itself, but the kind of swampy stream typical of the Delta. The stems of a papyrus thicket tower over this scene, creating a rhythmic pattern of striations in the background. Yet amid this balance and beauty, danger lurks: nests of birds in the thicket are threatened by mongooses climbing the plant stems, and in the water hippopotamuses threaten to overturn the boats of Ti and his boatmen, who aim spears at the animals and grapple them with ropes. By representing these dangers, and his calm mastery over them, in the offering chapel

A nobleman named Ti, shown larger-than-life in a marsh landscape. From his tomb at Saqqara, Egypt, *c.* 2400 BC.

of his tomb, Ti invited the image to protect his burial place, even as he communicated his own status near the top of a social order that sustained itself with such assertions about how privilege and power could keep Egypt safe.

The riverscape was not only a place of lurking disaster, of course. Its marshlands teemed with life, moisture and dense greenery that brought pleasure to mind. The banks of streams in the Delta, or the marshes of the Nile Valley, gave Egyptian poets and artists a setting in which to imagine flirtations and other forms of recreation enjoyed by the leisured elite. Here was humour and amusement in a holiday atmosphere – one went to the marshes to enjoy a 'beautiful day', code for drinking and love-making – but with a serious undercurrent in the core belief that the Nile was the origin of all life and all creation. Nor did the ancient Egyptian people go to excessive lengths to try to control the uncontrollable river: some monuments and temples were designed to embrace the flood, letting the Nile waters flow around and even through them. Better known today as the Colossi of Memnon, two colossal statues of King Amenhotep III bathed in the life-giving flow of the Nile when it was in flood, as did the entire temple (now destroyed) that they once fronted.[2] A picturesque view of this scene at sunset, painted in the early twentieth century, gives a rather romantic impression of the effect this intentional flooding had. It was an apt solution, given that the purpose of the now-lost temple was to help keep the spirit and memory of the dead king alive. The Nile held the power of both life and death, making it as mysterious as

David Roberts, *Statues of Memnon at Thebes*, 1846–9, lithograph. The 'Colossi of Memnon' – quartzite statues of King Amenhotep III, *c.* 1375 BC – are shown here at sunset, Luxor, Egypt.

its source to the ancient Greeks and Romans who visited Egypt or simply imagined it from afar.

Death and the Nile

The wind-eroded, water-lapped statues of Amenhotep III on the West Bank of Thebes (modern Luxor) earned a new name, the Colossi of Memnon, when Greek visitors identified them with the Trojan War hero Memnon, an Ethiopian king and son of Eos, the goddess of dawn. The historian Strabo, writing in the late first century BC, described visiting the statues at dawn with his friend Aelius Gallus, the Roman Prefect (governor) of Egypt.[3] The statue on the north side, which stands to the right when facing the pair, was believed to make a singing sound after sunrise, as if Memnon were greeting his mother. Most likely, an earthquake in 27 or 26 BC had further damaged the quartzite blocks that comprise the statue, and moisture evaporating in the early sunshine made a soft whistle or whine. In his *Geography*, Strabo confirmed that he heard a noise 'like a slight blowing', but he was less convinced that it came from the colossus. Nonetheless, the impressive statues remained a must-see for visitors in Roman times, as more than a hundred Greek and Latin inscriptions on the lap and legs of the statues attest. Although known as graffiti, most of these inscriptions are not hastily scrawled tags but carefully composed and carved records of a visit. Some are poems, like the two credited to Julia Balbilla, a Roman noblewoman who accompanied the emperor Hadrian and his wife Sabina to see – and hear – the statues in AD 130.

Balbilla seems to have shared with Hadrian an interest in the distant past, in particular the history of Egypt and the Near East; she herself was the descendant of Hellenistic kings in Syria. But for Hadrian, his interest in Egypt took on particular significance when his boyfriend, a handsome young man named Antinous, died during the journey.[4] The circumstances are unclear, but Antinous is thought to have drowned in the Nile. In Egypt, at least in Ptolemaic and Roman times (earlier evidence is mixed), victims of drowning were thought to become divine. For example, the tomb of a young girl named Isidora, which resembles a miniature Greek temple at the cemetery of Tuna el-Gebel, includes a long poem in Greek composed by her father, mourning her loss but taking comfort from his belief that drowning has turned his daughter into a water nymph with the gift of eternal life. Perhaps inspired by such ideas, Hadrian declared that Antinous was a god and that statues and cults for him should be set up throughout the Roman Empire. At his villa outside Rome, Hadrian recreated part of their Egyptian journey by building a long, ornamental pool called the Canopus, after the seaport near Alexandria.

For visitors who came to Egypt in Roman times, predominantly from the eastern Mediterranean, any risks posed by Nile travel were far outweighed by the appeal of seeing such sights as the Colossi and royal tombs at Thebes, and temples at Abydos and Philae, which were a focus of religious pilgrimage thanks to the worship of Egyptian gods throughout the empire.[5] The Nile cataracts at Aswan, including the islands of Philae and Elephantine, likewise appealed to travellers, who were impressed by the force and roar of the rushing water. The river originated in caves or grottoes somewhere in distant Ethiopia, it was thought, but its ultimate source remained a mystery akin to the other mysteries that ancient Egyptian priests kept secret among themselves. At the city of Praeneste, or Palestrina, in the hills east of Rome, a man-made cave housed a spectacular floor mosaic that represented the Nile from its secret source to its Delta mouth.[6] The mosaic was discovered and removed in the early seventeenth century, leaving scholars today uncertain about its specific setting, but it appears to have been part of the city's thriving forum in the second or early first century BC, at least several decades before the Roman conquest of Egypt. Water may have been channelled to drip over the mosaic, emphasizing its watery theme, and the details of the monuments, people, flora and fauna the mosaic represents must have struck Roman viewers as exotic yet informative at the same time. The curved part of the mosaic sat in the most distant part of the cave and represents the Ethiopian mountains. Sailboats, temples in both Greek and Egyptian style, and hippopotamuses and crocodiles mark the course of the river, seen at flood height, as it winds its way to the front edge of the mosaic, where it meets the sea. Soldiers

Floor mosaic depicting life along the Nile River, from a grotto at Palestrina, Italy, *c.* 100 BC.

in Greek or Roman helmets gather under a draped, columned hall, while white-robed, shaven-headed Egyptian priests carry divine emblems.

The enticing details of this riverine world captured the Roman imagination of Egypt – and later imaginings as well, for the bird's-eye view of the Nile's course finds an echo in the engraved frontispiece to the *Description de l'Égypte*. The river and the ancient monuments along its banks epitomized an unchanging Egypt. Surely the Nile had always flooded, farmers had always sown and ploughed the land, and boats had always drifted downstream and sailed upstream with ease? This idealized view glided over changes in how the land and water were managed, however, and the question of who owned them, not to mention changes in the environment as the course of the river shifted or its tributaries silted up. By the time the first volume of the *Description* appeared in 1809, even more changes were underway as Egypt's new ruling dynasty turned to Europe to help navigate Egypt into the modern, industrial age.

The Nile blues

After Napoleon's defeat by the British, an Ottoman general of Albanian parentage, named Mohamed Ali, stepped in to fill the power vacuum left in Egypt, which remained part of the Ottoman Empire. Under his long period of rule as governor (*wali*) of the country, Mohamed Ali introduced substantial changes to develop Egypt's infrastructure, often by inviting European expertise and investment. He assumed ownership of almost all the arable land in Egypt and sought ways to maximize its output. In particular, he followed French advice to plant a variety of long-staple cotton in the Delta, laying the foundation for Egypt's important textile industry. Under Mohamed Ali, a new canal was also dug between Cairo and Alexandria, making it easier for boats to transport goods between the two cities and thus facilitating ever-increasing exchanges with Europe and the rest of the Mediterranean.

After his death in 1848, Mohamed Ali's nephews, sons and grandsons carried on with programmes of modernization, which allowed European powers like Britain and France to gain a colonial toehold in the Egyptian economy. British firms contracted to build railways in Egypt, while the French architect Ferdinand de Lesseps, whose father had supported Mohamed Ali's dealings with the French government, won a contract (over British protests) to build the Suez Canal that would link the Mediterranean to the Red Sea. By the 1860s Egypt was booming. The cotton crop turned a substantial profit when the American Civil War disrupted supply from the southern plantations, and work on the Suez Canal and its new port city of Ismailia blazed ahead, in time for the grand official opening in November 1869. But behind these outward successes lay a system of state monopolies, heavy taxation and forced or exploitative labour, requiring peasants to work on state-funded projects like new irrigation channels, the Suez Canal itself and the expanding railway network. In the south of the country, irrigation projects focused on providing water for sugar cane crops, which fed the sugar factories owned by Egypt's rulers (now upgraded to *khedives*, viceroys) and their families. A similar pattern of intensive farming and industrial monopoly shaped cotton agriculture in the north, although the cotton industry declined in the 1870s when better-quality American cotton returned to the market. Coupled with the usual worries about flood levels – 1863 saw the worst flood of the century – these changes to water and land management made the lives of Egypt's rural population even harder, and their subsistence more tenuous.

That is why there is an uncomfortable irony in the way Western visitors to nineteenth-century Egypt insisted on the timeless character of the river views they enjoyed. Tourism itself was a product of modernization and growing colonial influence. European and American advisers, industrialists and investors based themselves for short or long stays in the country, as did Greek and Levantine merchants and bankers, including many Jewish firms. Steamship services cut the journey time across the Mediterranean, while improved rail links made it straightforward to reach Cairo from Alexandria or Ismailia. On the Nile itself, tourists could travel by *dahabiya*, a sail-rigged boat with a few cabins, usually hired privately with its own Egyptian crew, or from the 1870s by steam-driven paddleboat. The British firm of Thomas Cook led the way in organized tourism, using paddle steamers to take larger numbers of visitors up and down the Nile. So reliable and well established were Cook's Tours that in 1884 the British Government asked the company to organize the expedition to relieve General Gordon in the Anglo-Egyptian Sudan. Cook's moved 18,000 troops, 40,000 tons of supplies and 40,000 tons of coal from Newcastle to Egypt to supply the 27 steamers that made the journey to Khartoum. Some 650 sailboats and 5,000 Egyptian men were also involved in the expedition, which ended in a major setback for the British army when Gordon was killed, but which is a salient reminder that tourism in Egypt was a sideline to the colonial exploitation of Egypt and Sudan for military, commercial and industrial purposes.

Many of the sites Victorian and later tourists visited are the same ones tourists have continued to visit ever since, especially in Upper Egypt: Aswan (where the Cataract Hotel was a favourite of Agatha Christie) and, time permitting, travel beyond the first cataract to sites like Abu Simbel and Wadi Halfa; the Graeco-Roman temples at Edfu, Esna and (north of Luxor) Dendera; and the sites on both banks of the Nile at Luxor, where the Winter Palace Hotel was the most prestigious address. Stopping along the Nile in Middle Egypt – Mallawi, Amarna, Asyut and Abydos – was also recommended, but since the 1980s tourism in the region has been disrupted due to security concerns relating to sectarian violence between its Muslim and Christian populations. In the nineteenth and early twentieth centuries tourists devoted more time to Alexandria and Cairo than many do today, including the mosques, medieval gates and churches of Old Cairo. And whereas river travel, sometimes combined with a rail journey, defined the tourist experience for a century, air travel means that tourists can now reach Luxor and Abu Simbel without setting foot on a boat or even stopping over in Cairo. Nile cruises remain a popular option, but most only ply the stretch of river between Aswan and Luxor. Overnight journeys by small felucca sailboats, pictured in the advertising for many Nile cruises, are a more basic option, suited to adventure-minded travellers.

If these changes to tourism have made the Nile something to look at from the banks or cruise in a short burst, rather than travel

Antonio Beato, photograph of a tourist steamboat on the Nile, *c.* 1898.

along at a leisurely pace, the river itself has been changed by a series of engineering works, culminating in the construction of the Aswan High Dam, which began operating in 1970. When the British occupied Egypt in 1882 and took control of the country's finances, one of their priorities was being able to regulate the Nile flood waters, minimizing the risk of damage or drought and thus maximizing agricultural revenue. In the first decade of the twentieth century they built barrages at Esna and Asyut to assist with irrigation in Upper and Middle Egypt. These lock systems followed on from the first dam project at Aswan, which was completed in 1902. When the height proved inadequate to handle high floods, it was raised again between 1907 and 1912, at which point a survey of archaeological monuments was also undertaken. The timing was apt, because the British government was reasserting its control (at the time, jointly with Egypt) over neighbouring Sudan. Egyptologists, artists and writers of the day spoke out against the effect the higher dam would have on archaeological sites in the area when its reservoir reached peak levels, submerging the temples on the island of Philae, for instance.[7] British engineers underpinned the worst-affected structures, but long exposure to water was bound to erode the sandstone and wash away vividly painted details.

In the 1950s, with the confidence of a revolutionary regime, President Gamal Abdel Nasser's government began planning a new, much larger Aswan dam project to generate the levels of electric power Egypt needed to continue its post-war development. The impact of the High Dam, as it became known, exceeded the concerns that previous dam projects had caused. Not only were temples like Philae and Abu Simbel, and hundreds of other known archaeological sites, due to be submerged under the lake the new dam would create, Lake Nasser would also cover long-established towns and villages, leading to the displacement of tens of thousands of people known collectively as Nubians, after the region of Nubia encompassing the southern border of Egypt and northern Sudan. To rehouse indigenous Nubians, new villages were built around Aswan, but far from the river. Communities lost their cohesion and their livelihoods, since many had relied on income from date harvests but lost their mature trees to the backed-up Nile. The knock-on effects of the forced migration are still felt among Nubians in Egypt today.

Rehousing the region's ancient temples proved to be a more straightforward operation, despite the tremendous costs and engineering feats involved. The Egyptian and Sudanese governments turned to the United Nations Educational, Scientific and Cultural Organization (UNESCO) to coordinate an international effort that involved surveying endangered archaeological sites in the area, conducting test excavations where possible and, most spectacularly, executing the wholesale removal of eighteen endangered temples dating from the 18th Dynasty to the Roman period. The largest and most famous were the adjacent temples honouring Ramses II and his queen, Nefertari, cut into the cliff face at Abu Simbel – the same temples depicted in the lithograph that hung over Freud's consulting couch in Vienna. The temples were sawn into blocks weighing up to 30 tons and re-erected against an artificial mountain on higher ground, some 65 metres above and 200 metres behind their original location. Their original alignment was maintained as much as possible, so that the rising sun can reach the inner chapel of the Ramses II temple on two days each year, illuminating a statue of the king and the gods, their arms entwined, for a few hours in February and October. The project was completed in 1968, having cost the then-staggering sum of $40 million.[8] Five other groups of relocated temples were also created in the region and, for smaller chapels, in the gardens of the Khartoum museum. As a thank you to nations that had contributed funds and expertise, Egypt donated four small temples to the United States, the Netherlands, Italy and Spain, each of which now stands in a museum or, in Madrid, a park near the Plaza de España. The rescued Nubian temples feature on the list of world heritage sites maintained by UNESCO – but impressive as their rescue was, they draw attention to some of the more troubling aspects of the 'world heritage' concept. What made the temples more valuable than villages and date palms, and to what extent has 'world heritage' favoured sites and monuments with particular meaning for Western culture?

EGYPT

Today, visitors to Abu Simbel who enter the false mountain behind the temples will confront the contrast between old and new. From the front, however, the temples appear to have been sited beside the modern lake forever, looking just as they did in 1817 after Italian engineer-turned-archaeologist Giovanni Belzoni bartered with local officials to secure the services of workmen. At least eighty men laboured to clear tons of drifted sand away from the temple facades, a task that remained incomplete until Belzoni could return to finish the work the following July, which that year corresponded to the holy month of Ramadan, marked by a daytime fast. Belzoni, at least, considered the physical strain worthwhile, for when he entered the main temple he marvelled at its vast halls and impressive supporting pillars in the form of royal statues. It was difficult to make drawings because the stifling heat made sweat pour onto the paper and ink, but Belzoni described walls covered with battle scenes and hieroglyphs, 'the style of which is somewhat superior, or at least bolder, than that of any others in Egypt'.⁹ This task complete, Belzoni and his companions sailed downstream, where they would undertake other clearance work (including the transport of the Kingston Lacy obelisk) over the next two years, before crossing the Mediterranean en route to London. There, Belzoni's published words and engravings made from those sweat-stained illustrations brought Abu Simbel to the attention of European audiences primed for news of all things ancient Egyptian.

To other cultures, from ancient Greece to the days of Belzoni and beyond, the Nile and its once-predictable flood seemed to summarize all that was distinctive about life along the great river in Egypt. Since the 1960s the Aswan High Dam has changed that significantly. The end of the annual flood has forced farmers to rely on expensive chemical fertilizers, which leave deposits of salt in the agricultural land; with no inundation to wash the salt away, ever more fertilizer is required to maintain productivity. Other changes extend further back in time, such as the British-built barrages of the late nineteenth and early twentieth centuries and the system of irrigation canals that enabled intensive agriculture on lands that Mohamed Ali had turned into his family's private property. Tourists may enjoy the romantic fantasy that their Nile journeys are a timeless legacy of the distant past, but history tells us that much has changed. Rather than assume that the past and the present are one unchanging stream, we should look with even more attention to how the ancient Egyptians represented their world.

FIVE

WALKING LIKE AN EGYPTIAN

In his classic book *Art and Illusion*, first published in 1960 and never out of print, the eminent art historian Ernst Gombrich used a *New Yorker* cartoon from 1955 to open his discussion of how different artistic styles over time have tried to represent the world just as it looks in human vision.[1] In the cartoon a group of young men, all bald-headed and wearing pleated skirts, are in a life-drawing class preparing to draw the model on the platform in front of them: a slender woman depicted by cartoonist Alain in recognizable Egyptian form, with her legs, arm and face in profile. To Gombrich, the cartoon captured a fundamental difference between Egyptian art and artists and the artists of the Greek tradition that Renaissance Europe inherited. Western artists tried to draw what they observed with their own eyes, while Egyptian artists drew what they had been trained to draw, a schema for representing 'the world' in a way that bore little resemblance to visual perception. The humour of the *New Yorker* cartoon is that we know Egyptian women did not look like the stiffly twisted, striding model, and that Egyptian artists did not train from life-drawing, squinting down their arms at their pencils to gauge proportions and perspective. The joke is on us, for ever assuming that 'our' way of making pictures is the only way, or that it was possible – in the words of The Bangles' pop song – to walk like an Egyptian.

Art historians of Gombrich's generation, however, did give priority to the lifelike, illusionistic representation favoured by ancient Greek and Roman art and by Renaissance and later European artists. The idea that the more closely a work of art resembles what it represents, the better the artwork is (and the more talented the artist, too) is an idea that has a powerful, pervasive hold on our collective imagination. We all know someone who dislikes Cubism, Abstract Expressionism or just about any contemporary art because such art is not figurative, that is, it does not depict human or animal figures, landscapes or anything else from the natural world in a 'natural' way. But what is 'natural' for art changes across times and cultures. When their work debuted in nineteenth-century France, the Impressionist painters were decried for their failure to represent the world accurately. All those fuzzy outlines and pastel hues, easily read today as scenic views and water lily ponds, were a radical departure at the time. How much more alien, then, the art of ancient Egypt seemed to be, together with the art of many other ancient cultures – Babylonia, Assyria, pre-Classical Greece, India and all the pre-Columbian societies of Meso- and South America.

Flip the history of art around, though, and the trickery of naturalistic or lifelike art turns Classical Greece and its imitators into the odd ones out. To represent the world as our eyes perceive it, painters and mosaic artists had to foreshorten parts of the image meant to be closer to the viewer, shade some surfaces to convey volume, and make figures or buildings in the distance smaller in relation to the foreground; you can see this in the Herculaneum fresco of Egyptian priests and the Palestrina mosaic of the Nile. In sculpture, the *contrapposto* posture, in which subjects shifted their weight onto one leg, creating a sense of motion through the body, made statues look almost like living bodies trapped in molten metal or turned to stone. These choices reflect specific historical circumstances and cultural values in, for instance, fifth-century BC Athens or early imperial Rome. The conventions that Egyptian artists used were also a conscious choice, made early in Egyptian history and carefully preserved and transmitted for millennia. In the same way that we recognize art that looks Egyptian, so, it seems, did ancient audiences. When Egypt was an influential power and an exporter of desirable goods, artists elsewhere copied Egyptian styles, and when Egypt became a Greek kingdom and then part of the Roman Empire, artists combined Egyptian forms of representation and architecture with the naturalistic forms that then held sway. It is not only Gombrich, or cartoonist Alain, who could spot the difference between two competing systems for turning the world around us, and within us, into a picture.

Nevertheless, an artist in the time of Cleopatra would not 'get' the *New Yorker* cartoon, because its absurdities are distinctly modern: the male artists and the female model, the institution of life-drawing classes, and the telling details – palm trees, chair shapes, kilts – that Alain used to indicate the setting as ancient Egypt. In this chapter we begin by considering what made Egyptian art look Egyptian to ancient eyes, and why it stuck with certain conventions in architecture, two-dimensional paintings and reliefs, and three-dimensional sculpture. Turning to European ideas about ancient Egyptian art, we pick up with the impact of the Napoleonic expedition and the early nineteenth-century opening of Egypt to Western visitors. How artists and designers used Egyptian-inspired decoration, architectural elements and subjects reveals how firmly ancient Egypt was fixed in the Western imagination as a sign of the mysterious, the mighty and the exotic Other, even when its art was admired for a certain delicacy or beauty. Nowhere is this tension between East and West, strangeness and beauty, stilted and lifelike, more apparent than in representations of Cleopatra herself, the queen whose shared Greek and Egyptian identities exemplify the quandary of what it has meant in the modern world to have 'lost' this ancient past.

Looking like an Egyptian

The female model in the *New Yorker* cartoon looks similar to the bronze plaque of the Nile-god Hapi, which we saw in the previous chapter, or the figure of lady Tabakenkhonsu, painted on her funerary stela (see p. 12). The figures face left, with the face in profile, the shoulders almost squared to the viewer, and the arms and legs also in profile, one foot in front of the other. Look more closely, and it is clear that several areas of the body – the stomach and belly button, the line of the back and buttock, those impossible shoulders and single-breasted chest – do not correspond to how a real body would appear in real space. Instead, they are indications of the body: lines and curves that link the head, torso and limbs together in a coherent whole that reads 'male' or 'female', 'human' or 'divine'. Like hieroglyphs, these figures could also be flipped around to face right. In fact, right-facing was the ideal orientation for Egyptian images, as it was for written texts; the three-line prayer on the bottom of Tabakenkhonsu's stela reads from right to left, for instance. But to make it possible for images and texts to be arranged on left and right walls in a room, or the left and right sides of a statue, reversibility was essential.

If the bronze Hapi, lady Tabakenkhonsu or the god Thoth, who holds her hand, were flipped to face right, the forward leg would be each figure's left leg, the one farthest from the viewer – like the feet of the goddess Nut as she fills the 'sky' of the painted wooden stela. In the scene of Tabakenkhonsu with Thoth, Isis and Osiris, short texts identifying each figure face in the same direction as that figure. From around the time the first pyramids were built, statues in Egypt always represent kings and high-ranking men standing with the left leg forward, probably inspired by the preferred orientation of hieroglyphs and other two-dimensional images, which had already been established. Egyptologists often refer to this pose for statues as the striding stance, because the advanced leg suggests that the figure is walking or about to step forward. Statues of women represent them with their feet together until the New Kingdom, when sculptors began to show some high-status women with the left foot advanced. By the Ptolemaic period, statues carved in traditional Egyptian style, often from dark Egyptian stones, used a confident striding stance to depict powerful queens such as Arsinoe II, Cleopatra III and Cleopatra VII (the famous one). One such statue, now in a museum belonging to the Rosicrucian Order in San Jose, California, dates to the first century BC and may represent either Cleopatra III or VII; without an inscription, it is impossible to say for certain.[2] Probably set up in an Egyptian temple, this granodiorite statue relied on stoneworking techniques that Egyptian masons had perfected over centuries. It represents the queen in a style that was intentionally old-fashioned, as a way to associate her with a long lineage of rulers from the distant Egyptian past.

Dark stone statue of a queen, probably Cleopatra VII, *c.* 40 BC.

Not only is her left leg far forward, more like a king than a queen, but her arms hang at her sides; queens usually had their left arm bent across the body. The tight curls of hair arranged in three stiff sections – one either side of the face, another down the back – echo the tripartite headdresses depicted on gods and goddesses, and the three cobras on the queen's forehead triple the conventional *uraeus*-symbol used for royalty; this was a new feature in the Ptolemaic period. The rounded belly, full breasts, and prominent nipples and navel may make it seem at first glance as if the queen is naked, but the hem of a dress stretches between her lower legs. A youthful, fertile, female body was a sign of beauty and perfection, although today it may seem a sharp contrast to the dour facial features, which are similar to portraits of Ptolemaic queens on their coinage and in marble statues made for them in the Greek style.

Egyptian architecture also had a distinctive style. Most buildings in ancient Egypt were mud-brick or mud-plastered reeds, not unlike the wattle-and-daub technique used in medieval Europe. But tremendous effort went into monumental stone architecture for tombs and temples, which is what survives to such an impressive extent today. From the New Kingdom onwards, temples were fronted by monumental gateways, often known by the Greek word *pylon*. The pylon controlled actual and symbolic access to the temple's forecourt and inner rooms, which were off-limits to anyone but priests and attendants in a state of ritual purity. A drawing by the Victorian designer Owen Jones depicts the facade of a temple pylon, although the scenes and inscriptions painted on it are only approximations, not direct copies. What Jones has right, though, is the sloping shape of the pylon walls, their flared top, known as a *cavetto* cornice, and the lashed detail all around their edges. The *cavetto* and lashings are echoes in stone of the floppy reed heads and bound reed stems used in simple mud-and-reed structures. Having this echo of the natural world – life-giving Nile-soaked earth and reeds – was important to Egyptian religious ideas about the temple representing the creation of the world and providing a home for the gods. Inside, temples had courtyards and roofed-over rooms supported by columns in the form of papyrus stems, another reference to the river.

The Jones drawing also correctly captures how colourful Egyptian art was. The walls and ceilings of temples were painted in rich colours, and even gilded in parts. Tombs and most statues were also painted, and to nineteenth-century viewers this colourful appearance was an intriguing contrast to the white marble statues and buildings of Greece and Rome (although we now know that those were once painted, too). When Owen Jones designed the Crystal Palace Exhibition in Hyde Park, London, in 1851, the vivid reds, blues and greens of the Egyptian court, which he co-created with Joseph Bonomi, formed a stark contrast to the cool white plaster casts in the Greek court beyond.[3] Both men had visited Egypt and both were artists, whose numerous sketches and water-colours of the ancient sites helped them lavish particular care on the Egyptian display in the Crystal Palace, which tens of millions of visitors, including Queen Victoria, saw both in Hyde Park and when the whole structure was re-erected at Sydenham, south London, in 1854. This was ancient Egypt tailored to Victorian taste, and any Egyptologist would quibble with the details. But Jones and Bonomi were not after accuracy so much as effect, and the symmetry,

Owen Jones, watercolour showing the entrance pylon of an Egyptian temple, 1833–4.

Philip Henry Delamotte, photograph of the Egyptian Court at the Crystal Palace exhibition, Sydenham, London, 1850s–60s.

rhythmic repetition and direction of the mock-temple conform to the spirit, if not the letter, of ancient artistic practice. The dominant figures – gods and goddesses – face towards the doorway, and a fecundity figure appears in the bottom band of one wall, which is exactly where such figures belonged in an Egyptian decorative scheme. The walls of tombs and temples, or drawings made on papyri, were always divided into horizontal bands, termed registers. From the top to the bottom of a wall (not visible in the photograph above), each register enforced a subtle hierarchy, and in a genuine tomb or temple chamber what belonged in each register and on each wall or doorframe had to fit together into a coherent whole. Rather than the life-drawing lampooned by cartoonist Alain, an Egyptian artist's training included structuring a programme of decoration, fitting figures and inscriptions together, and learning proportions, patterns and insignia by heart. In ancient Egypt, art was too powerful to leave to creative whim. If Egyptian art and architecture looked stilted or gaudy to some nineteenth-century viewers, others found it delightful, unusual or even alluring enough to put it to new use.

Decorating like an Egyptian

In the years after the Napoleonic expedition to Egypt, and especially after Vivant Denon published a popular account of his own involvement, a vogue for Egyptian-inspired interior design caused a small stir in Britain and continental Europe, especially France.[4] Always a niche taste – Egyptian-style furniture and tableware did not fit easily into the average home – this 'Egyptomania' confirmed that ancient Egypt appealed to European interests, but only at a certain remove. English designers like Thomas Hope offered drawing-room chairs with sphinx-shaped arms, and Josiah Wedgwood made a red-and-black tea service encircled with winged scarabs; a crocodile formed the teapot lid. Cupboards and clocks also had the Egyptian treatment. Chairs and teapots may have been novelty items, but cupboards and clocks perhaps suited an Egyptian theme: closed cupboards evoked secrets and security, while timepieces matched Egypt's deep antiquity and concern with endurance. A marble and gilt bronze clock by the London firm of Vulliamy & Son borrowed designs directly from Denon's account of his travels in Egypt. Four sphinxes support the clock face, which is mounted on a *cavetto*-cornice 'gateway' with battered sides and a winged sun-disc at the top.

By the late nineteenth century the development of tourism and archaeology in Egypt – both linked, as we have seen, to colonial and imperial interests in the country – meant that ever more accurate renderings of ancient monuments were available for consumption around the world, especially with the rise of photographic technology. Museums also filled their display cases with growing numbers of finds from archaeological excavations, since foreign excavators at the time were allowed to keep much of what they discovered. Whether through books, in museums or on their own travels, a widening audience could form ideas about ancient Egypt thanks in part to the more commonplace objects – baskets, vases, tools and jewellery – that archaeologists now saved, rather than the architectural fragments, statues and coffins that interested earlier collectors. Designers were attracted by the handmade elegance of Egyptian furniture. For instance, the Pre-Raphaelite painter William Holman Hunt designed ebony- and ivory-inlaid chairs closely inspired by ancient examples he had seen in the British Museum, down to the curve of the cane seat.[5] Holman Hunt had travelled to Palestine to help him paint works with a Christian theme, and he was friendly with members of the Arts and Crafts movement, which elevated handmade over factory-made goods. Here, then, was a gentler version of ancient Egypt than the overpowering architecture copied for cemeteries and Freemasons' halls (even a prison, in 1840s Philadelphia), or the over-the-top sculptures in the Crystal Palace.

The 'mania' in 'Egyptomania' implies that popular interest in Egyptian motifs for interior design, fashion or architecture was an uncontrollable, unpredictable urge. In contrast, no one characterized ornamentation inspired by the classical world as a craze – Wedgwood's cameo-effect china, Greek columns and architraves, replica Apollos and Venuses, all seemed entirely fitting in

Vulliamy & Son, mantle clock in Egyptian style, made in London, 1807–8.

Cast metal door guard in Egyptian style, on an apartment building in Bologna, late 19th century.

a domestic interior, country estate or cityscape. But the rediscovery and re-interpretation of ancient Greece and Rome had its own history and social significance, just as the different uses of ancient Egyptian art and architecture did. The crucial points at which Egyptian decor became a fad corresponded to historic events and the availability of sources, such as the Napoleonic expedition and Denon's book in the early 1800s, the Crystal Palace Exhibition and new Egyptian galleries at the British Museum in the 1850s, or the opening of the Suez Canal in 1869. Flushed with the success (and income) of the Canal project, *khedive* Ismail commissioned Giuseppe Verdi to compose the opera *Aida*, which inaugurated the Cairo opera house in 1871 – and may have helped inspire a fresh burst of Egyptian inspiration in Verdi's native Italy. Some producers and consumers of Egyptian-themed design had an interest in biblical history, or in Freemasonry, but whatever specific appeal the arts of ancient Egypt held, their general association with the marvellous and mysterious held sway. No matter how familiar it became, ancient Egypt kept a touch of the alien and other, which only a 'mania' could explain.

In the 1920s the discovery of the tomb of Tutankhamun launched another period of Egyptian fashion in home interiors, clothing and popular entertainment – 'Tut-mania', this time. In Britain, where the press covered the English-led excavation in detail, Huntley and Palmer biscuit manufacturers issued a biscuit tin in ancient Egyptian style, and a Lancashire textile firm printed furnishing fabrics with Egyptian motifs. The *Times* of London and other newspapers seized on the chairs and candle-holders, baskets and walking sticks, clothing and perfume pots in Tutankhamun's tomb to paint a picture of cosy domesticity for the boy-king, which the modern middle classes could recreate at home. This tame, Tut-friendly view of antiquity made for a convenient contrast with the post-First World War turmoil of the Middle East, where Egypt was struggling to free itself from British political and military domination. Egyptians seeking independence had clashed with the British army in 1919, and when free elections were finally held in Egypt in 1922, just months before the Tutankhamun discovery, the first prime minister was nationalist leader Sa'ad Zaghloul, whom Britain had twice sent into exile. Excavator Howard Carter, who had spent his entire working life in Egypt, misjudged the new mood when it came to the Tutankhamun discovery, granting exclusive access to the London *Times* and expecting to share objects from the tomb with his backers in England and New York. The Egyptian government, which included French and British employees, revoked his excavation permit for a year, exerting their own rights over the tomb and its reawakened pharaoh.[6]

Delicate prints, faux scarabs and glitzy biscuit or cigarette tins gave ancient Egypt the common touch, from Paris to Peoria, but as we will explore in later chapters, modern Egyptians and members of the African diaspora were beginning a long battle for greater recognition and social change. The singular features of ancient Egyptian designs could be adapted to many different uses and purposes, some frivolous, others with more serious intent. Nor were Egyptian-style architecture and decorative arts the only sphere in which this ancient culture's visual legacy was reshaped amid contemporary concerns. Since at least the early nineteenth century, fine artists (and later, photographers) had been representing the antiquities of Egypt as romantic, empty spaces ripe for colonial expansion, or as stage sets for exotic, and often erotic, glimpses of the past. Some of the most renowned painters of their day conjured up an ancient Egypt peopled by characters who were just like us, but not quite. This imagined Orient was a place of contradictions: old and new at the same time, familiar yet unfamiliar, too. Because many artists anchored their versions of ancient Egypt in surviving evidence, as Holman Hunt had done with his Egyptian chairs, their creative licence easily seems more real than the real thing, but it would be our mistake to confuse the two.

Painting ancient Egypt

The Dutch-born painter Lawrence Alma-Tadema kept a wooden couch in his London studio to use as a prop in his paintings. Now in the Victoria and Albert Museum in London, the couch had one long side and its pair of legs carved in Etruscan style, and the other side and its legs in Egyptian.[7] It served Alma-Tadema well in his lush, finely detailed oil paintings of ancient life, which earned him fame and fortune in Victorian Britain. Although scenes of Greece and Rome were his most popular subjects, Alma-Tadema painted several well-received scenes from Egypt and the Bible as well, such as the discovery of the infant Moses in the Nile. In addition to studio props like the couch, Alma-Tadema closely researched antiquities and ancient architectural features through books and museum visits. Recognizable details, combined with the expressive characters he painted, brought the ancient past to gleaming life under Alma-Tadema's brush. Or did it? The footstools and ostrich-feather fans looked authentic enough – but the blushing, pale-skinned women of his paintings, the occasional dark-skinned man for contrast, and the fresh, flower-filled spaces these figures occupied could only be a fantasy, a drawing-room version that filtered fragments of antiquity through Victorian taste.

Representing fictional or historical characters from ancient Egypt in the realistic style of Western art had an immediate visual impact in that it did away with the conventions of Egyptian art, whose human figures looked so stiff and regimented to modern viewers. Where the originals seemed remote and alien, the reconstructions that history-minded painters created managed to transport viewers back in time. Alma-Tadema's 1872 painting *The Egyptian Widow* combines his closely observed execution of Egyptian art and architecture with an imaginary scene of mourning, as the widow of the painting's title kneels weeping next to the mummy of her husband. In the background, five male musicians sit cross-legged on the floor, singing, shaking the tambourine-like *sistrum* or strumming a harp. The setting is an Egyptian temple

Lawrence Alma-Tadema, *The Egyptian Widow*, 1872, oil painting.

with elaborate papyrus-shaped columns and low walls that give a view onto a palm-filled courtyard beyond. Alma-Tadema was a master of detail: the *cavetto*-cornices, lashed edgings and rows of rearing cobras are close renderings of actual architectural features, as are the richly coloured column capitals. A basket on the floor, the wooden door panel, musical instruments and the altar-like arrangement of jars to the right (so-called canopic jars, used to hold mummified organs) are all based on objects Alma-Tadema could see in museums, especially the British Museum in London, where he had lived since 1870. It was in the museum's upstairs galleries, colloquially known as 'the mummy rooms', that he would have seen the coffin to the left of the widow, and the shrouded mummy shown lying on a wooden bier with the legs and tail of a lion. Both the coffin and the mummy date to the era of Roman rule in Egypt but use images of the gods in a purposely old-fashioned way. Alma-Tadema was not as interested in historical accuracy as these closely observed studies might suggest, however. He has combined a coffin and mummy from the second century AD with canopic jars from a thousand years earlier, and covered the temple walls with scenes from tombs a few hundred years earlier still. For Alma-Tadema and his audience, the interest lay instead in the overall effect of a 'real' ancient Egypt to support the emotive heart of the painting: a mourning widow, her face buried in her hands and her hair falling forward (like the mourners in Egyptian art), while the familiar bald-headed priests perform a funeral dirge. Our heart strings are being plucked as surely as the harp.

On the one hand, erasing the gap of time and space between an Egyptian temple and a Victorian art gallery encouraged empathy or identification with people from the ancient past, which we tend to take for granted as a positive effect. On the other hand, not only time and space were erased in this process: centuries of Egyptian history were erased as well, especially from the seventh-century introduction of Islam to the present day. Paintings with ancient Egyptian themes were part of a wider set of cultural signals that reinforced an artificial split between East and West, with ancient Egypt reserved for the enjoyment of white, Christian Europeans. And race did matter: the pale or tawny skin of the widow and four of the magicians makes an intentional contrast with the dark skin of the harpist. In the nineteenth century viewers were closely attuned to even subtle distinctions in gradations of skin tone and what they implied, in the dominant 'science' of the day, about racial identity, admixture and human progress.[8] Africa, the dark continent of the colonial imagination, seeped around the edges of ancient Egypt, a silent shadowing. To keep Egypt within the circuit of what was considered Western heritage, this Africa had to be kept in its place, wedged into a corner like the black harp player.

Such anxieties about race, belonging and the ownership of the Egyptian past were not spoken of directly. Instead, we glean them from what academics call discourse: the shared assumptions through which a society operates, which are created and communicated through visual experiences, writing, performance, commerce, science, political debate and so forth. These elements operate together, not separately. Thus painting ancient Egypt convincingly as a living past relied on the archaeological recovery of Egyptian antiquities, but it also made archaeology seem more important, even urgent, to conduct. At the same time, archaeology in Egypt expanded as Britain tightened its hold on the country following the 1882 invasion and establishment of a 'veiled protectorate'. In the 1890s several of Alma-Tadema's fellow history painters, including Edwin Long and Edward Poynter, joined forces with British archaeologists, military officers and politicians to campaign for the preservation and protection of ancient monuments in Egypt.[9] The threat they perceived came from two areas: the alleged neglect of antiquities by the Egyptian government that remained in place, since Egypt was part of the Ottoman Empire, and secondly its antiquities service, headed by French Egyptologists. There was also widespread concern about the new dam that the British planned to build at Aswan, which would permanently flood famous temples like the temple of Isis at Philae. In the eyes of the British campaigners, neither the French nor the Egyptians could be counted on to look after ancient Egyptian sites. Imagine the French and the Egyptians complaining about how Britain took care of Stonehenge, and the insult this implied, not to mention the diplomatic wrangling involved, becomes clear. Yet arrogant attitudes set a tone for debates around heritage in Egypt and the Middle East that still echo today. Who decides what counts as heritage, and how best to preserve it?

Claiming Cleopatra

Heritage is a word that carries considerable weight. It derives from the same Latin root that gives us 'inheritance', and until the twentieth century 'heritage' referred to property or responsibilities passed down through a family line, especially in legal terms. The idea of heritage as a significant aspect of culture shared by an entire group of people grew out of late twentieth-century moves to protect certain places, landscapes and artworks from development, war or natural disasters. Established in 1945, in the wake of the Second World War, UNESCO is perhaps the best-known arbiter and advocate of heritage today. UNESCO introduced a World Heritage List in 1978, which now includes more than a thousand buildings and monuments, conservation areas and examples of 'intangible' heritage, such as dance forms and craft skills.[10] The phrase 'world heritage' suggests that the preservation of anything designated as heritage is in everyone's interest, on the assumption that heritage has a universal value. But the fact that world heritage is managed by a United Nations organization, with official entrants nominated by member nations, reveals how closely our modern notion of 'heritage' is associated with the nation-building of the nineteenth, twentieth and (consider South Sudan) twenty-first centuries – and thus how closely what is 'heritage' depends on the interests of who is in charge, or wants to be.[11] Preserving an example of heritage, or destroying it, can both be effective ways for a regime, or its opposition, to legitimize its cause.

If heritage means that culture can be inherited, rather like a royal throne or the shape of a nose, then it can also be fiercely fought over, like any inheritance. Competing cultural memories of ancient Egypt are today often framed as heritage debates, thanks to the dominance of the heritage idea – or indeed, ideal. Yet the movement of people, objects and ideas over the centuries makes it difficult to pinpoint whose heritage anything derived from ancient Egypt is. According to the nation-state model, since the culture of ancient Egypt originated in what is now the country of Egypt, modern Egypt and it inhabitants have a priority claim. Yet museums in London and Berlin reject the idea that 'star' objects in their museums – the Rosetta Stone and the bust of Nefertiti – should return to Egypt, and if the Egyptian government decided to raze the pyramids to the ground, there would be an international outcry. Where people take heritage to be less about a nation state and more about kinship and lineage, more quandaries emerge. Are modern Egyptians overly removed from their ancient ancestors by virtue of being predominantly Muslim? This is the argument many people of European descent have made since the eighteenth century, informing the discourse of Orientalism. Ancient Egypt was an early home of Christianity and Judaism, not to mention a major centre of Greek learning and philosophy; hence Europeans considered it 'Western' by right. Expanding the idea of the ancient population to include more of the African continent opens still another line of argument. To see ancient Egypt as fundamentally African – many Greek writers referred to it as Ethiopia, after all – allowed people elsewhere in Africa or of African descent to identify the history and culture of Egyptian antiquity as their heritage, too.

Debates concerning heritage often crystallize around high-profile objects (the Rosetta Stone), monuments (the pyramids) or figures – like the famous Cleopatra, a queen who knew a thing or two herself about the inheritance of a throne and the shape of a nose. The French scientist and philosopher Blaise Pascal remarked that had her nose been shorter – in seventeenth-century thought, a sign of weak character – the face of the world would have been different. And indeed, the political confrontation between Cleopatra and Rome changed the course of history, bringing all of North Africa and the eastern Mediterranean under Roman sway. Cleopatra has fascinated artists and writers for centuries because, like ancient Egypt itself, she seemed to be two things at once.

At the time of her defeat, Roman poets called her a whore and a monster, vilifying her as a woman whose feminine wiles led Antony astray and her country into ruin. Like Helen of Troy, a mythical figure, Cleopatra represented the danger a beautiful woman posed to male-dominated order, while the luxury and learning of her Hellenistic court was met with envy and suspicion in the Roman republic. Much of what we know about Cleopatra was written many years after her death, for instance in the lives (moralizing biographies) of Julius Caesar and Mark Antony composed by the Greek writer Plutarch around AD 100.[12] Rediscovered and translated during the Renaissance, Plutarch and other Greek and Latin authors were the only sources Europeans had for the life or looks of the queen for many years. Marble portraits of her in the

William Wetmore Story, *Cleopatra*, marble sculpture, modelled 1858, carved 1860.

classical style were only identified as such in the twentieth century, based on comparison to her coin portraits. In the late 1990s some scholars identified the dark stone statue in the Rosicrucian Museum as a statue of Cleopatra, too, although the lack of inscription makes it impossible to know for certain. What is important is that there would have been many statues of Cleopatra VII in Egyptian as well as classical style, in her home country, none of which necessarily show us what she looked like in real life. She also appeared in Egyptian form on temples she supported, on her own behalf and that of her son (by Julius Caesar) and co-ruler, Ptolemy XV Caesarion. Egyptian sources and cultural memories in Egypt itself preserved strikingly different ideas about Cleopatra than the Roman and later Western notion of her as a scheming sexpot: Arab historians remember the queen for her wisdom, great learning and achievements on behalf of her country.[13]

When the American sculptor William Wetmore Story chose Cleopatra as a subject in the 1850s, he did so without knowing any of these ancient images, only the posthumous Greek and Latin accounts.[14] In his studio in Rome, Story specialized in Neoclassical sculpture, and his *Cleopatra* is one of several near-life-size statues he designed representing legendary or historical women in contemplative moments. Like other sculptors of his day, Story created a clay or plaster model for stonemasons to carve in fine Italian marble, hence several similar versions of the *Cleopatra* exist, made over several years. When the sculpture was first exhibited, viewers admired its authentic Egyptian detail: the striped cloth head-covering the queen wears is Story's version of the pharaonic *nemes*, with a cobra (*uraeus*) over the brow, and on each wrist the queen has an Egyptian-inspired bracelet with scarabs and snakes. The deep folds of the dress and the way it slips off the queen's shoulder, revealing one breast, may bring a hint of enticing Orientalism to the statue, but the bare breast also alludes to Cleopatra's suicide, since convention had it that she held a poisonous snake to her chest to receive the fatal bite. Particularly striking to Story's American audience in the 1850s and 1860s, however, were the queen's strongly modelled facial features, with a large, straight nose, cleft chin and firm, full lips. Contemporary viewers took these features as signs of Cleopatra's 'Ethiopian', that is African, identity. Story belonged to a prominent Boston family who were active in the abolitionist movement. His anti-slavery sympathies, and those of his audience in the northern United States, stressed the grave decision faced by Cleopatra and, by extension, the American nation as it weighed its options in the years leading up to the American Civil War. Cleopatra as an African queen, faced with a desperate choice, was a work of art that predominantly white audiences could interpret as ennobling slaves of African descent, whose future, and America's, hung in the balance.

Few viewers of Story's *Cleopatra* today would read its facial features and white marble as African, Ethiopian or black. Art endures, societies change. Viewers are more likely to take the marble queen in her Egyptian headdress as a whitewashing of Cleopatra, denying her the African-ness many people now see as central to this historical figure's identity. Perhaps the dark stone statue in the Rosicrucian Museum, with its serious demeanour and confident Egyptian stride, seems more securely black and African because of its outward appearance, an Egyptian Cleopatra rather than a Greek or American one – but even it has a tenuous identity: possibly Cleopatra vii, possibly one of her regal predecessors. Made almost two thousand years apart, neither statue is transparent in our contemporary world, though analysing the context in which the statues were first made and used can go some way towards helping us understand their makers' original intent. Cleopatra was and is mutable, like any aspect of the long-lost past. We can never find her, only traces of her glimpsed in an occluded glass. Not-quite-naked and not-yet-dead, Cleopatra fits a fantasy 'ancient Egypt' that is of very modern making.

SIX

VIPERS, VIXENS AND THE VENGEFUL DEAD

Associated with one of the most alluring figures from Egyptian history, the contrasting statues that closed the last chapter indicate the gulf between ancient and modern ideas of queenship. Cleopatra's suicide after her defeat by Rome often marks the 'end' of ancient Egyptian civilization in conventional chronologies. Since her reign post-dates Manetho's *Aegyptiaca*, this is a dividing line modern scholars have drawn, based on a distinction between Egypt as a country governed from its own territory and Egypt as a province answerable to central powers elsewhere. This distinction owes much to ideas of nationhood formed in the eighteenth century and applied, violently, in the nineteenth century and ever since. In the transition from Ptolemaic to Roman rule, however, the violence we remember most today is the violence of Cleopatra – and Antony – against themselves, through their suicides. To the victor goes the claim of restoring and maintaining peace.

With its heady mix of sex and death, the Cleopatra legend is revealing for what it says about Western attitudes to Egypt – and to women. Any well-known historical personage will be interpreted in different ways over time, but Cleopatra's alleged sexual bewitching of respectable Roman men has had an especially powerful hold over cultural imaginations. Her suicide is the comeuppance for a woman so intelligent that she could (almost) succeed in a man's world, and so beguiling that men were powerless to resist her. Misogyny seeps through this spin on the bare historical facts. Cleopatra's womanhood had already been used against her in the propagandistic Roman accounts that circulated during her lifetime and just after her death, written by poets and politicos loyal to the one-time Octavian, newly declared *princeps* and later emperor Augustus. Some of these slanderous and salacious attacks had been familiar to European audiences since the Renaissance, as had more circumspect, but still colourful, episodes of her biography relayed by the Greek scholar Plutarch in his lives of Julius Caesar and Mark Antony, which were written around AD 100. As a woman and a foreigner, Cleopatra did not warrant her own 'life'. To the victor goes also the right to write history.

This chapter takes Cleopatra as a starting point for considering how it is that sexpots, sorcerers and mummies have come to dominate our recovery of a 'lost' ancient Egypt, especially over the past 150 years. While historical evidence and archaeological finds contribute to ideas about Egypt – the discovery of Tutankhamun's tomb, for instance, or the supposed DNA identification of mummified bodies – different eras seem to get the ancient Egypt they desire, or deserve. The literary scholar Edward Said characterized colonial-era European discourse about North Africa, the Middle East and South Asia as Orientalism, an imagined conception of 'the Orient' that constructed these places and their inhabitants as everything opposite to how Western cultures saw themselves: lazy where the West was hard-working, dirty where the West was sanitized, disorganized where the West was efficient, trapped in time where the West was modern, and morally suspect where the West was disciplined in matters both sexual and pecuniary.[1] While Said's critique has been challenged or refined in many ways over the years, its central tenet is valuable for reminding us that we have inherited stereotypes about the ancient and more recent pasts of Egypt (and elsewhere) that reflect the concerns of the dominant powers of the day. For every voracious queen and bare-breasted goddess, egomaniacal pharaoh or rampaging linen-wrapped corpse, we should be asking, whose story, what evidence, and why did it appear on our cultural horizon when it did? Perhaps losing ancient Egypt has led us to find parts of ourselves we might be better off without.

The beautiful and the dead

The vogue for paintings inspired by ancient Egypt, like those of Alma-Tadema, Poynter and Long, was not limited to Britain by any means. It was widespread throughout Europe and wherever artists trained in European-style painting. Scenes from ancient history were often a sideline of painters who specialized in the so-called Orientalist style (the nineteenth-century term repurposed by Said), which favoured North African and Middle Eastern subjects such as crowded, crumbling streetscapes; markets, mosques or desert caravans; and the ever-popular harem or *hammam*, both of which offered an excuse for painting naked women. These subjects owed just as much to painters' imaginations as did their depictions of ancient Egypt or the Holy Land. No one painted the new railway stations of Cairo and Damascus, for instance, or upper-class Egyptian ladies dressed in the latest Parisian fashion. Like the props in Alma-Tadema's studio or the antiquities he studied for his paintings, time could be mixed and matched or shifted around, so that Egypt was never allowed to be as modern or 'advanced' as the West – and for women, even royal women like Cleopatra, clothing was optional.

European artists had been depicting Cleopatra for centuries, and earlier images of her make for an interesting contrast with later versions in the Orientalist mode. With little direct knowledge of Egyptian sites or antiquities to go on, painters tended to treat Cleopatra as they would any other figure from ancient history. Both her suicide, recounted by Plutarch, and her love of luxury, emphasized by Pliny the Elder, inspired the choice of scenes. The seventeenth-century Bolognese painter Guido Reni painted several versions of Cleopatra gazing heavenward as she clasped an asp to her décolleté, but he also used Cleopatra as a portrait mode for the wives of patrons who no doubt wished to be associated with her vast wealth. About 1744 Giambattista Tiepolo painted a cycle of frescoes showing episodes of Cleopatra's life from both Pliny and Plutarch. Decorating the reception hall of the Palazzo Labia, Venice, these frescoes likewise emphasized the Egyptian queen's riches and munificence, a luxury to which the successful merchants of this key trading port with the East could easily aspire. Tiepolo depicted Cleopatra, and all the other figures in the frescoes, as a noblewoman of his present day, elaborately costumed, coiffed and bejewelled. The only gesture to the ancient setting of the scenes was the Classical architecture, fitting to the genre of history paintings in the eighteenth century and to the era in which Cleopatra lived.

Before the Napoleonic expedition and subsequent opening of Egypt, artists in Europe had had few references for ancient Egyptian buildings and works of art, apart from obelisks, a few sculptures and small objects in old princely collections. As we saw in the last chapter, the appearance of Vivant Denon's travel account, and many others, provided ample source material for artists to copy and adapt, as did the eventual publication of the *Description*. Artists who travelled to Egypt themselves – like David Roberts, whose paintings sold well as prints, or Owen Jones and Joseph Bonomi, designers of the Crystal Palace's Egyptian court – not only furthered wider public ideas about what ancient Egypt (or what was left of it) looked like, but they added to the visual 'library' of sand-drifted temples and hieroglyphic excess. No surprise, then, that artists began to exploit this material to depict Egyptian subjects, including Cleopatra. Yet paintings from around the 1830s onwards went much further, operating in the new Orientalist mode to depict the ancient world in an exotic register that rendered it not so much timeless as atemporal, removed from historical time altogether.

In the Orientalist imagination, the Middle East and its ancient pasts were ripe for fantasy: bourgeois, heterosexual male fantasy in particular. Titillating canvases were a speciality of one of the most prolific and renowned of the Orientalist painters, Jean-Léon Gérôme. Gérôme also painted Classical myths and scenes from French history, including several commemorating Napoleon's Egyptian campaign, as the disgraced emperor's reputation revived during the Second French Empire of Napoleon III. But his paintings of 'Oriental' subjects, such as snake-charmers, desert scenes, slave markets and Turkish baths, were Gérôme's most popular, especially since the 'slaves' and bathers were invariably beautiful, light-skinned, nude women. For his painting *Cleopatra before Caesar*, exhibited at the Paris Salon in 1866, Gérôme depicted an episode from the Greek scholar Plutarch's account of Julius Caesar's career. Plutarch recounted the first meeting between Caesar, a Roman politician and general, and Cleopatra VII, the Ptolemaic queen who was then embroiled in a civil war with her brother and co-ruler of Egypt, Ptolemy XIII. Rome had long intervened in the dynastic struggles of the Ptolemaic kings and queens, and in 47 BC Caesar came to Egypt to turn the conflict to Rome's advantage. According to Plutarch, the teenaged Cleopatra had herself smuggled past Caesar's guards in a cloth sack, so that she could meet with him in person and plead her case. Later translations turned

Engraving after a detail of Jean-Léon Gérôme, *Cleopatra and Caesar*, 1866, oil on canvas.

the sack into a 'carpet', hence Gérôme painted the young queen surrounded by an Oriental rug – and wearing a dress that leaves the royal breasts entirely bare. What Roman general could resist?

Other painters used Cleopatra's suicide as the basis for revealing this tempting flesh, painted creamy white in contrast to her dark hair and eyes, making the queen an 'Oriental' beauty on the pale end of the spectrum to which nineteenth-century artists were so attuned. In the Gérôme, for instance, Cleopatra's light skin and petite features contrast with the dark skin, heavy brow and protruding jaw of the servant who has carried her in the carpet roll, and whose African features matched nineteenth-century expectations of servitude. Suicide scenes sometimes created a similar opposition between Cleopatra and her female attendants, Iras and Charmian. The two could be shown as dark and 'Egyptian' in contrast to the queen, or as light-skinned and 'Greek' like Cleopatra. In Jean-André Rixens' *The Death of Cleopatra*, first exhibited in 1874, the painter adopts a middle way, painting Cleopatra with whiter skin than her slightly more tawny handmaidens but leaving us to question whether this is because she is more 'Greek' than they are – or because she is dead. On a gilded bed florid with Egyptian swags and carvings, the gleaming body of the queen lies

Jean-André Rixens, *The Death of Cleopatra*, 1874, oil on canvas.

inexplicably naked save for her jewellery and hair adornments. Displayed for viewers like a lurid trophy, the posthumous version of the living humiliation Cleopatra feared at Roman hands, the last of the Hellenistic monarchs is reduced to a dead yet delectable body. In this Orientalist-influenced history painting, Rixens engages with the long cultural lineage of the Cleopatra legend and its artistic representations. But his dead, not dying, queen should also be seen within the context of those other dead Egyptian bodies that had been revealed to view with increasing focus and frequency over the course of the preceding century: mummies, whose own allure shifted from the sexual to the sinister the more invested Western powers became in modern Egypt's body politic.

Unwrapping the dead

What happened to the corpse of the historical Cleopatra remains a mystery. Her fellow Ptolemaic dynasts had adopted some version of the embalming and wrapping treatments perfected in Egypt for the ritual mummification of the dead, especially the ruling classes and influential elites. The Ptolemies' Macedonian precursor, Alexander the Great, had already been embalmed in some form when he died on campaign in Persia. His friend Ptolemy, founder of Cleopatra's dynasty, diverted the leader's body to the city Alexander had founded in Egypt, Alexandria, and it is possible that some sort of dynastic tomb on the eastern outskirts of the city housed the burials of the royal family, and perhaps even Alexander himself.[2] When Octavian entered Alexandria after Cleopatra's death, he is reported to have visited Alexander's tomb but declined to view the Ptolemaic crypts, dismissing them as unworthy of his attention and thus aligning himself instead with the glorious victories of Alexander. Whatever Octavian permitted as funeral rites for the defeated queen, Cleopatra's body does not survive, only the images artists have conjured over the centuries.

Plenty of other bodies did survive from ancient Egypt, however, thanks to the use of mummification. The practice of arresting the decay of the corpse by desiccating it, anointing it with oil and wrapping it in linen had been a hallmark of Egyptian civilization since ancient times, and today mummies are one of the first things the word 'Egypt' conjures in people's minds. In the fifth century BC Herodotus appears to have seen bodies before they were wrapped, or else older examples unwrapped for his benefit, since he comments on the astonishing preservation of their facial features, down to the eyelashes. With information gleaned from the Egyptians he spoke to (in Greek) Herodotus outlined three methods of mummification based on different price bands.[3] The most costly process involved eviscerating the corpse through a slit the embalming priests made in the left side of the abdomen; the embalmers extracted brain tissue through the nasal cavity. The corpse was then packed in a salt compound called natron, which formed on evaporated salt lakes in the desert fringes, and the desiccated body was packed and coated with sweet-smelling, resin-infused oils. The final part of the process involved wrapping the corpse finger by finger and limb by limb in several dozen layers of linen bandages, pads and sheets of cloth – some of which, we now know, derived from the clothing the deceased had worn in life and cloths used to wrap divine statues in local temples. Many Egyptian garments comprised wrapped skirts, dresses and mantles, and wrapping or dressing the statues of the gods was the focus of the daily ritual priests carried out for them, so that the statue would have fresh clothing each day.[4] In less expensive versions of embalming, Herodotus wrote, less effort went into both the wrapping and embalming stages; one option was to inject turpentine into the abdomen through the anus, with the effect of partly dissolving the inner organs and slowing down decomposition.

Herodotus' *Histories* circulated widely in the ancient world and, since their rediscovery in the early sixteenth century, throughout Europe and beyond. His account of mummification thus exerted a powerful influence on ideas about ancient Egypt and about this distinctive practice, as did the Old Testament tale of Joseph, whose elderly father joined him in Egypt and was embalmed and buried with Egyptian rites. Such an elaborate treatment of the dead body (the entire process took seventy days) and the efforts apparently made to preserve the corpse in a lifelike form, contrasted sharply with Islamic, Jewish and Christian burial practices. In medieval and early modern times, mummies had a value beyond this curiosity, however, because ground-up mummy was recommended for medicinal use. Medieval Arabic scholars such as Avicenna (Ibn Sina, who died in 1037) recommended *mummia* for almost everything, although Avicenna himself did not stipulate Egyptian *mummia* for the purpose.[5] Dissolved in liquid, the *mummia* (from the Persian for bitumen) was swallowed as a treatment for stomach and liver disorders in particular. A brisk trade in *mummia* operated between Europe and the Middle East, with ancient body parts extracted from the cemeteries around Cairo and pulverized. There was ample scope for trickery, too, using fresh corpses hastily 'mummified' and coated in bitumen or pitch to meet demand. Rumours were rife about criminals' executed bodies being pickled, dried and ground to be passed off as the authentic article. Such suspicions about adulteration of the product led several doctors and writers in Europe to decry the practice of *mummia* consumption, which began to fall from fashion in the seventeenth century. Ingesting *mummia* amounted to cannibalism, always an uncomfortable thought. It also commoditized the human body, a concern raised for the contemporary slave trade as well. As the eminent English physician Sir Thomas Browne put it, 'Mummy is become merchandise, Mizraim [Egypt] cures wounds, and Pharaoh is sold for balsam.'[6] Browne wondered where this exploitation of the dead would eventually lead, if left unchecked.

It was no coincidence that one of the first recorded mummy unwrappings and dismemberings to take place on European soil was undertaken by the German pharmacist Christian Hertzog, in Gotha in 1718.[7] Mummies had been collectors' items since the sixteenth century, when the Italian adventurer Pietro Della Valle recounted his explorations in the Saqqara cemeteries near Cairo, where he chiselled 'bitumen' (in fact, hardened resin) off a mummi-fied head and brought two beautifully decorated, wrapped-up mummies back with him. In the noble and princely collections known as cabinets of curiosity (*Wunderkammern*), mummies – both human and animal – were prized specimens. The painter Peter Paul Rubens owned one, and Athanasius Kircher avidly studied, through drawings and correspondence, a mummy in the collection of the

Grand Duke of Tuscany.[8] In 1705 the English surgeon Thomas Greenhill made a close study of all the available literature on mummification to date in hopes of proving that embalming was 'no less ancient and noble than Surgery itself'.[9] Greenhill thought the English should adopt the practice for hygienic reasons and that surgeons, rather than undertakers, were best qualified to perform it for aristocratic clients.

As medical training became more structured and professionalized over the course of the eighteenth century, access to corpses for anatomical investigation became more important. Understanding the inner workings of the human body united surgeons and physicians, who otherwise had distinct identities. At the same time, natural scientists began to consider human difference in the far-flung regions that European colonialism encountered. Egypt sat at the juncture of Africa, the Middle East and the Mediterranean, and it was well known to educated Europeans through ancient Greek and Roman authors. Where the ancient Egyptians, in particular, fit into the emerging 'science' of race was a question that anatomists proved eager to explore in the late eighteenth and early nineteenth centuries, exactly the time when the Napoleonic expedition had made the supply of antiquities (and mummies) from Egypt much easier, and more desirable. Leading scientists of the day, including Johann Friedrich Blumenbach in Germany and Georges Cuvier in France, drew different conclusions about the supposed racial identity of the ancient Egyptians: closer to the Caucasian race, thought Cuvier; Ethiopian, argued Blumenbach, using one of the terms applied to African peoples in these early schemes.

The idea of different races and fixed racial characteristics soon led to the creation of a hierarchy whereby some races were superior to others: the basis of what became scientific racism, a 'science' put to sinister use. In the early nineteenth century successful campaigns against the slave trade created an environment in which, paradoxically, scientific racism became entrenched, for instance among advocates of a slave-based economy in the southern United States. Slave-owners and some scientists seized on racial classification to justify the enslavement of Africans, who were deemed less intelligent and considered 'childlike' or 'primitive'. The most extreme form of this argument was the theory of polygenesis, which held that humans were not a single race, but several. In the 1850s the American Egyptologist George R. Gliddon, who had spent much of his life in Egypt, and the Alabama physician and slave-owner Josiah Nott published a multi-volume book called *Types of Mankind*, which went into several printings in the decade leading up to the American Civil War.[10] Nott and Gliddon used not only the skulls of mummies but examples of ancient Egyptian art to argue that the ancient Egyptians were a Caucasian society that used black, African ('Negroid') slaves as a workforce, from domestic servants to physical labourers. The American South was heir, in this view, not only to the Classical cultures of Greece and Rome – think of all those columned plantation houses – but to the great civilization of Egypt, which it deemed a slave-holding society parallel to its own.

It might be reassuring to imagine that these race-based interpretations of ancient Egyptian civilization were fringe ideas, but so pervasive were assumptions about human differences in the nineteenth century that no area of cultural life was immune from them, including the academic study of the past. Comparative anatomy informed all studies of humankind, from biology and anthropology to history and archaeology. Physical differences between humans were mapped against perceived cultural differences to create schemes of progress, with asserted European or Caucasian accomplishments always coming out on top. It is important to understand how widely accepted ideas about anatomy, mummies and race were in Egyptology and archaeology, which established themselves as full-fledged academic disciplines in the latter nineteenth century. One of the founding fathers of the discipline, W. M. Flinders Petrie, actively engaged with physical anthropology research, collecting skulls from his fieldwork to send to colleagues in the UK, including the eugenicist Francis Galton.[11] The rest of the bodies he found were reburied en masse at excavation sites, and the same is true for other excavations of the time. Petrie used the results of anatomical analyses to concoct race-based theories, such as his idea that prehistoric Egyptian civilization had only attained a certain level of accomplishment – late in the Naqada period – when a 'Dynastic Race' of people from the Levant moved into the Nile Valley and introduced innovations in materials, technologies and societal organization. In other words, the influence of a northern 'race' superior to the indigenous population was essential to any advance in forming the society Petrie and other Egyptologists recognized as 'ancient Egypt'. Petrie also compiled a photographic dossier of ancient Egyptian art representing the different cultural groups the Egyptians had encountered, from the Libyan deserts, Nubia and the upper reaches of the Nile, and the Levantine coast and Anatolia. In ancient Egypt, especially during its own period of military and trade expansion in the New Kingdom, visual representations of different 'types' were an essential contrast to the Egyptian elite's representation of themselves. These Libyan, African and West Asian peoples were also the conventional enemies of the Egyptian pharaoh, who trampled them underfoot and bashed them over the head in innumerable artistic scenes. Ancient Egyptians had their own 'others' – but to try to make their constructions of difference correspond to our own invites false comparisons, though it does say something about the long history of how societies divide themselves into 'us' and 'them'.

The unwrapping and anatomical investigation of mummies reached its peak in the late nineteenth and early twentieth centuries, corresponding to peaks both in the intensity of archaeological investigation in Egypt and in the widespread interest in investigating racial typologies, sexual characteristics and traces of disease. In the years around 1910 the Australian-born professor of anatomy Grafton Elliot Smith carried out exhaustive studies of the mummified bodies of many famous pharaohs, queens and priests, who had been found re-buried in caches in the Deir el-Bahri cliffs and the Valley of the Kings. He defended his research, and the ethical dilemmas it raised, in the preface to his published catalogue, arguing that 'modern archaeologists, in doing what they have done, have been rescuing these mummies from the destructive vandalism of the modern descendants of . . . ancient grave-plunderers. Having these valuable historical "documents" in our possession it is surely our duty to read them as fully and as carefully as possible.'[12]

In the catalogue of the mummies, where he 'let the naked bodies tell their own story', Smith's scientific language created an aura of authority and objectivity, as it was intended to, but read in close detail his observations on the skin colour of the mummies, the high-bridged (that is, Caucasian) noses of the Ramesside kings, the breast size and shape of various queens, and the treatment of the genitals of female mummies make for difficult reading today, if we approach them with a more critical and questioning eye.[13]

Like other anatomists who worked on mummies, Smith was a product of his age: but what assumptions did that age bring to bear on their research, and how has it continued to influence our own perceptions? Even the idea that mummies should be unwrapped and dissected could be called into question, though it was rarely questioned at the time, and then only where royal mummies were concerned, because they were royal. Few Egyptologists paid much attention to the copious linen wrappings, which were often discarded after the investigation, yet these wrappings were one of the most expensive and significant aspects of the ancient ritual. When examining the condition of the embalmed corpse, for instance when looking for traces of the natron salt, embalming oils, or evisceration and excerebration, the influence of Herodotus loomed large over the anatomist's table. Smith and others characterized variations from the 'norm', or poor preservation of the body, as laziness or incompetence on the part of the embalmers, Orientalizing the ancient Egyptian workers as feckless or financially unscrupulous. If we consider the mummification process in the light of Egyptian ritual evidence, however, a different picture emerges; what goes unsaid or unrecorded becomes a significant point of silence. Tellingly, for instance, the ancient Egyptians themselves say nothing about how to treat the body, while there are extensive descriptions of how to wrap and arrange the linen, and what kind of linen it should be. We also know that the application of purifying, cleansing natron, sweet-smelling resinous oils and freshly woven linen, both to statues and to dead bodies, was held to reawaken them and restore them to life. The idea that the body beneath the linen, which no one but the priests ever saw, was the most significant part of the process and had to be as 'lifelike' as possible, casts our own assumptions backwards in time. The end result was what mattered to ancient Egyptians, and it was meant to be hidden away, secured, protected, inviolable and beyond all human view. Unwrapping the dead went against everything the ancient Egyptians called for in their prayers and ritual texts, as was well known. Small wonder, then, that some anxiety should begin to show about whether the mummies hauled out of their tombs and placed under the surgical knife might some day seek revenge.

The haunted past

The exotic and the erotic have tinged modern imaginings of ancient Egypt with the glow of Orientalism, not only in the fine arts we considered at the start of this chapter, but in the theatre and cinema, public exhibitions, advertising and literature, from the lowbrow to belles-lettres. The world of scholarship does not exist in isolation, and whether it took place in Egypt or in the new research institutes set up across Europe and North America, academic Egyptology was, and remains, in dialogue with these other ancient Egypts. Archaeologists working in Egypt courted press attention to help inform the public about their discoveries, and also to promote their work and emphasize their own authority as interpreters of the past. In turn, press coverage, publications and exhibitions were the visual fodder for wider receptions of ancient Egypt, based on historical figures and facts and recent archaeological discoveries. The scholarly and the scintillating always intertwined: the French Egyptologist Auguste Mariette helped with the scenario for Giuseppe Verdi's ancient Egypt-set opera *Aida*, which premiered in Cairo in 1871, while the German Egyptologist Georg Ebers authored a number of popular romances set in ancient Egypt, to bring the finds of his colleagues to greater attention and bring their historical context to life. Between the 1860s and 1890s, Ebers was widely read in his native Germany and his works, including *An Egyptian Princess*, *The Bride of the Nile* and *Cleopatra*, were translated into other European languages, too.

Ebers's romantic novels made suitable reading for ladies, but other works of fiction inspired by ancient Egypt toyed with headier

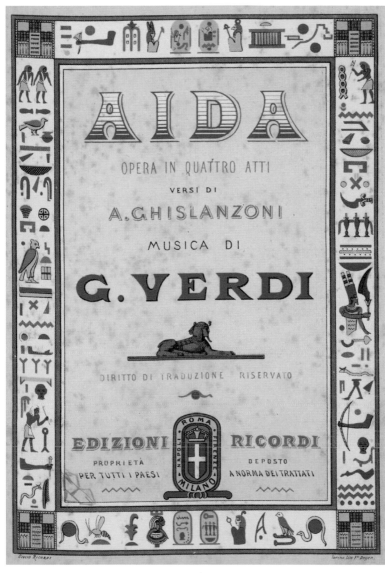

Cover of a vocal score for Giuseppe Verdi's *Aida*, 1872.

themes of death and sex. Orientalism in art and writing developed out of the Romantic movement in the 1830s, a 'back to nature' – or back to the distant past – reaction to the upheavals of the Napoleonic wars, in which the self-styled artistic temperament sought inspiration from the natural world, far-flung travel or direct encounters with art and ruins linked to antiquity. The French novelist and playwright Théophile Gautier turned his hand to ancient Egyptian themes, inspired by his own travels as well as those of his friend Maxime Du Camp, who visited Egypt from 1849 to 1851 on a photographic expedition organized by the French ministry of education. One of Gautier's short stories, first published in the 1830s, recounted a stolen night Cleopatra enjoys with an Egyptian servant while Mark Antony is away. Cleopatra longs for passion to counteract the land of the dead over which she rules, an Orientalizing trope for Egypt's long decline as a country and for the death-obsessed myth of mummification.

Cleopatra is the sexual predator in the story, initiating her encounter with 'the native'. Usually it was a European, male protagonist who sought out the 'Oriental' woman, although he might also find himself pursued by the desires of the long-dead. Another Gautier short story, 'The Mummy's Foot', set the action in a Paris junk shop, which a young man-about-town, an aspiring writer, visits in search of a paperweight for his desk.[14] The elderly shopkeeper, who looks like 'an Oriental or Jewish type', rummages through the shop's astonishing array of bric-a-brac – Hindu gods, Mexican fetish figures, Malayan weaponry – before the writer spots a 'charming' foot, which he at first mistakes for a piece of ancient bronze sculpture, polished to a gleam by thousands of kisses. Closer inspection reveals that the foot is embalmed and unwrapped, with a faint impression of the bandages in the surface of the skin. The merchant tells him that the foot belonged to an Egyptian princess named Hermonthis – and warns him that her father, the pharaoh, would not be pleased to see it turned into a paperweight.

Undaunted, the young man returns home and proudly places his new purchase on top of a pile of his unfinished writing, to 'charming, bizarre, and romantic' effect. That night, after a drunken meal with friends, he enters his apartment to find that

> a vague whiff of Oriental perfume delicately titillated my olfactory nerves. The heat of the room had warmed the natron, bitumen, and myrrh in which the *paraschistes*, who cut open the bodies of the dead, had bathed the corpse of the princess.

It was a perfume at once sweet and penetrating, a perfume that four thousand years had not been able to dissipate. The Dream of Egypt was Eternity. Her odours have the solidity of granite and endure as long.

In his heavy, champagne-induced and perfume-ridden sleep, the writer dreams that he sees the foot scuttling and jumping across his desk. His bed curtains open to reveal a young woman 'of a very deep coffee-brown complexion', with almond-shaped eyes but a nose 'almost Greek in its delicacy'. The woman and her missing appendage strike up a conversation, in which the foot informs Princess Hermonthis that it has been sold by 'the Arab' who robbed her tomb. At this, the writer – still in a dream – relinquishes his ownership of the foot, which the princess happily fits back onto her leg. The writer and the princess travel as if by magic to an ancient Egyptian underworld, where her father, the king, rejects the writer's marriage proposal on the grounds that the Frenchman is too soft, too mortal. Finally the writer is abruptly awoken to find that in place of the mummified foot, the Egyptian amulet that Hermonthis wore in his dream now sits on his desk: a much safer, if less exciting, paperweight.

Such gothic adventures are undoubtedly entertaining, and Gautier's tongue may be in his cheek as he describes his fictional alter ego's adventure with the slender-footed princess. However, stories like 'The Mummy's Foot' betray the extent to which stereotypes of the ancient and modern Middle East are embedded in the foundations of our contemporary world.[15] Readers shrink now from the racist characterization of the shopkeeper as 'an Oriental or Jewish type', yet the idea of the thieving, untrustworthy Arab is alive and well, from successful Hollywood films like *The Mummy* franchise to right-wing news commentary on political and military unrest in Arab regions, where antiquities are increasingly under threat – arguably at least in part because of the bitter histories that associate them with Western concerns. In the story, the writer is powerless to resist the lure of Egypt, which acts on him through its perfume, its sheer endurance, and of course its beautiful women, whose dark complexions and almost-Greek noses combine the exotic and familiar, like ancient Egypt itself. How surprisingly little some things have changed, given that today's museum gift shops stock 'Egyptian'-inspired scents for the home and 'Oriental' glass bottles for perfume.

Other things did change, of course, and as Egypt became a cause of financial and military concern for Europe's imperial powers, its fictionalized mummies began to turn more threatening than the amiable Princess Hermonthis.[16] In the late nineteenth century, following Britain's invasion and occupation of Egypt, British (at that time including Irish) authors as diverse as Bram Stoker, Arthur Conan Doyle and Rudyard Kipling began to depict archaeological encounters with ancient Egyptian remains less as a source of sensual enticement and more as a haunting with malevolent intent. With its veils lifted and its shrouds unwrapped, the Egyptian mummy began to fight back against its violators in fiction, just as contemporary Egyptians were demanding less interference from foreign interlopers in real life. Confidence in the values and justice of British imperialism may have been unwavering on the surface, but tales of endangered excavations, doomed adventures and cursed disturbances speak to the anxieties simmering underneath.

No writer exemplified this genre more than H. Rider Haggard, who drew on his early career in South Africa, then a British colony, to write immensely successful stories and novels set in colonial locales, including *King Solomon's Mines*, *She* and its sequel, *Ayesha*. Rider Haggard popularized the 'lost world' genre, a precursor of science fiction in which contemporary characters discover an ancient culture living in isolation, entirely cut off from the outside world and its way of life thus preserved. It should have been the archaeologist's dream – but often became the stuff of nightmare. The act of breaching this present past disturbed the balance of the lost civilization, unleashing its dark forces on the British protagonists and their loyal, native servants. In *She* a Cambridge professor and his ward, handsome blond Leo, stumble across a remote African civilization of dark-skinned people ruled by the white-skinned queen Ayesha, known as 'She-who-must-be-obeyed'. Ayesha has lived for two millennia using her magical power, and in Leo she thinks she has found the reincarnation of her Greek-Egyptian

An inscribed potsherd made by H. Rider Haggard's sister to match the plot of his best-selling novel *She*, published in 1887.

lover, Kallikrates, whom she once killed in a fit of rage. Beautiful but poisoned by lust and vengeance, Ayesha gets her inevitable, fatal comeuppance in the end – at least until Rider Haggard brought her back to life in the sequel. To complicate matters further, Leo turns out to be a descendant of Kallikrates and the Egyptian priestess Amenartes, who wrote out their ill-fated story on a potsherd – which Rider Haggard had recreated, and which his family later donated to their local museum in Norwich Castle. The character of Leo, the quintessential Englishman, is thus an ancient Egyptian with a bit of Greek blood for good measure, while Ayesha, the white-skinned queen, is the wilful oppressor of her African people.

Questions of race were central to the Victorian world-view – and no less complicated for it.

Another Rider Haggard story, 'Smith and the Pharaohs', combines romance, archaeology and mystery in the setting of two famous museum collections of Egyptian antiquities: the British Museum in London and the Egyptian Antiquities Museum in Cairo, which had recently moved to the building it still occupies in Tahrir (then Ismailia) Square.[17] First published in *The Strand Magazine* in 1913, the story echoes reservations that Rider Haggard himself expressed about the excavation, unwrapping and display of Egyptian mummies, and of royal mummies in particular. The eponymous Smith is a successful businessman who ducks into the British Museum to escape the rain and falls head over heels for the sculpture of an ancient Egyptian woman, mounted on a gallery wall. Informed that the sculpture is a cast, and the original ('Mariette found it, I believe, at Karnac') is in Cairo, Smith immerses himself in Egyptology and journeys to Egypt to train with archaeologists there. Eventually granted his own excavation permit under the usual terms, namely that the antiquities department could keep whatever they wished, Smith commences work at Thebes and muses under the moonlight:

> The mystery of Egypt entered his soul and oppressed him. How much dead majesty lay in the hill upon which he stood? Were they all really dead, he wondered, or were those *fellaheen* right? Did their spirits still come forth at night and wander through the land where once they ruled?

Smith's efforts are rewarded with the discovery of the tomb of the beautiful – and fictional – 18th Dynasty queen Ma-mee, though the royal mummy is missing apart from one elegant, bejewelled hand, which Smith wraps safely and stores in a cigar box. Back in Cairo, Smith discusses the find with both the French head of the antiquities service and the museum director, also French: Rider Haggard was clearly well informed about how archaeology worked in Egypt, from his own research, travels and acquaintance with British Egyptologists. After their meeting, Smith wanders the halls of the museum, ruminating again as he studies the royal mummies on display. So absorbed in his reflections that he misses closing time, Smith has to spend the night asleep in the museum with the mummies where, like the hero of Gautier's story, he too dreams of ancient Egypt. The rulers of Egypt, from Menes to Cleopatra, address him, to ask his help in avenging the violation of their tombs – until the mummified hand in his pocket clatters to the floor, revealing Smith as no better than a thief himself. With the help of Queen Ma-mee, whose hand it is, after all, Smith defends himself against this charge by arguing that it was his love for ancient Egypt that led him to excavate and to preserve his discoveries in the museum. The pharaohs let Smith off the hook: his violation was done in 'reverent ignorance', and the real thief, they decide, is the Egyptian priest who first broached Ma-mee's tomb with greed and lust in mind. When Smith awakens, he finds on his finger a gold ring with Ma-mee's name and knows that they were lovers in the past, now separated forever. Smith, consequently, abandons Egyptology.

In this story Rider Haggard questions the aims and methods of archaeology even as he accepts their essential premise, for the immortal love between Smith and Ma-mee asserts a Western or British 'right' to possess Egypt just as strongly as archaeology did. The long-lost queen – beautiful and sweetly perfumed, of course – exists most vividly in Smith's dream vision, but in reality she survives through the objects displayed in London and Cairo, without which Smith would never have encountered (or re-encountered) her. The pharaohs themselves absolve Smith of conscious wrongdoing in his archaeological research, blaming instead another Egyptian through the menacing figure of the priest. At the end of the story, Smith – and Rider Haggard – professes uncertainty over what exactly happened that night in the museum. But the seed of doubt was planted: what did the Egyptians – ancient and modern – think of these foreigners poking around in their business?

Harry Burton, photograph of the antechamber of Tutankhamun's tomb taken shortly after its discovery, December 1922.

The curse of Tutankhamun

The First World War reconfigured the eastern Mediterranean and the Middle East forever, as the victorious powers unstitched the old Ottoman Empire. In 1919 both peaceful and violent protests accompanied Egyptian attempts to negotiate self-rule, which met with limited success. Rather than continue negotiations, the British government unilaterally granted limited powers to the Egyptian government in 1922. Egypt's first free elections swept a nationalist political party, the Wafd, to power just months before Howard Carter discovered the tomb of Tutankhamun. At a time of pitched politics, the astonishing discovery of an almost untouched royal tomb seemed like the stuff of fiction and was embraced fervently in the Western press as much as within Egypt. To the newly independent state, the reawakened Tutankhamun was a powerful symbol of the Egyptian nation reawakening after centuries of rule from outside, and Egyptian poets wrote paeans to the boy-king, which we consider further in Chapter Eight.

But amid the excitement of the find, tensions quickly arose around the immediate issue of who should represent it in the press:

Carter and his patron, Lord Carnarvon, or the Egyptian antiquities officials? In the background loomed the larger issue of whether the finds from the tomb would wind up in the Cairo museum or be divided between Cairo and Carnarvon. Times had changed faster than Carter and Carnarvon realized, and the days were long past when the Egyptian government, including the antiquities service still headed by French specialists, would yield such a major discovery to a foreign collector.[18] The first photographs taken inside the tomb hinted at the 'wonderful things' that filled the first room – and at the treasures behind the sealed doorway waiting to be found. Tourists flocked to the scene and famous visitors, including Rider Haggard, enjoyed personal tours of the work in progress, although their presence inevitably disrupted progress on the work itself.

When Carnarvon, weakened by years of ill health, succumbed to sepsis in April 1923, just as the first season of excavation was drawing to a close, the Western press had decades of fictional and political drama to call on in painting his death as Tutankhamun's revenge, the 'curse of the pharaohs' writ large. This personal tragedy did nothing to smooth over the tensions brewing between Carter and the antiquities department as work on the tomb progressed, which centred on the preferential access Carnarvon and Carter gave to the London *Times*. Finally, just after he had raised the lid of the royal sarcophagus in the second excavation season, Carter downed tools and the antiquities department reclaimed control of the tomb. After a year's break – and a change of government in Egypt, more acquiescent to British interests – Carter and his team returned to work. By the time the royal mummy was ready to be unwrapped, press coverage had become, mercifully, more subdued. Carter led calls to treat the royal remains with 'reverence', mindful of the new political landscape as well as the specific concerns that had always surrounded the treatment of royal bodies, as if they were more deserving of careful treatment than any other mummified remains. In fact, the remains of the king had to be chiselled bit-by-bit out of his coffin, where the wrappings were stuck fast with resin. To extricate the heavy gold mummy mask, Carter and his colleagues detached the head from the body and used heated knives to prise it from the mask. The hands were detached to remove the royal rings and bracelets, and the lower legs, feet and pelvic bones likewise, since all were photographed separately.

In the autumn of 1926 the disarticulated mummy of Tutankhamun was rearranged in a tray of sand, rewrapped and replaced in its sarcophagus, within the otherwise emptied burial chamber of the tomb. It was intended, finally, to be an eternal rest for the boy-king – but both the mummy and the alleged curse would be brought back into the light repeatedly in the coming decades.[19] Each time someone associated with the original excavation died, their lifespan was measured against the likelihood of pharaonic interference, and a series of blockbuster museum exhibitions in the 1970s and the 2000s sparked new theories about Tutankhamun's life and legacy. Tutankhamun's mummy is still in the tomb, but not in the sarcophagus, out of sight. In 2007 the Egyptian authorities installed a specially commissioned museum case in the burial chamber, so that the remains could be displayed in a climate-controlled environment. Any curse, it would appear, is on Tutankhamun himself, who cannot rest, thanks to the lost civilization he now represents.

SEVEN

OUT OF AFRICA

Two glimpses of ancient Egypt through the lens of contemporary media: first, right-wing news magnate Rupert Murdoch's Twitter account, where in November 2014, he felt moved to comment on the Hollywood blockbuster *Exodus: Gods and Kings*, which some Twitter users and web bloggers had criticized for its all-white cast. 'Since when are Egyptians not white?', tweeted Murdoch, adding that all the Egyptians of his acquaintance were. Glimpse two, the pop star Rihanna's Instagram feed in 2012, where the much-tattooed singer revealed her latest ink: the goddess Isis with outstretched wings, the sweeping lines of which follow exactly the curved underside of Rihanna's breasts. Rihanna also has two other ancient Egyptian-themed tattoos (the bust of Nefertiti, on the left side of her ribs, and a falcon on her left ankle), among other 'exotic' inkings such as Arabic, Sanskrit and Tibetan expressions. Rihanna herself has commented only that the winged Isis commemorates the death of her 'guardian angel' grandmother, but some Rihanna-watchers associate the Isis and Nefertiti tattoos with the singer's black identity: one African beauty adorning her body with others.

Since many people who would identify as white also have ancient Egyptian tattoos, reading race into Rihanna's choices exemplifies the pigeonholing to which black – and female – artists are so often subject. But taken together with Murdoch's tweet (which plenty of other Twitter users lampooned), the possibility that an ancient Egyptian-themed tattoo might refer to black or African heritage speaks volumes about how large the issue of race looms in our own society, and how intrinsically ancient Egypt is entangled in it. Rupert Murdoch is happy to identify the modern Egyptians of his acquaintance as being just-like-him in racial terms, and many people in North Africa and the Middle East do have pale skin and blue eyes, two of the physical attributes associated with a 'white' or Caucasian racial phenotype. Egyptians themselves distinguish different skin tones, facial features and hair textures, for instance identifying darker skin tones with the southern reaches of the country (conventionally seen as rural and backwards, like hillbillies in American lore), and the very darkest skin tones with Nubia near the border with Sudan. The cultural weight given to these kinds of distinctions is another matter, however. Difference translates into prejudice and inequity where factors like economic exploitation have shaped power dynamics within and between societies. Decades after the break-up of empires and the overthrow of racist regimes in the American South and Apartheid South Africa, deep-rooted anxieties about race are a fact of contemporary life, and ancient Egypt is their proving ground.

By this point, readers might be able to anticipate my own observation here: more than personal identities or idiosyncrasies, it is cultural memory – and forgetfulness – that determines what someone assumes an ancient Egyptian looked like, or why anyone, of any identity, wants an ancient Egyptian deity inked into her skin. More than any other lost civilization, ancient Egypt inspires heated debates about race, and for good historical reasons: when the concept of human racial differences was first formulated in Europe in the late eighteenth century, European powers were eyeing up Egypt's strategic position between the Mediterranean and the Red Sea. At the same time, European thought had begun to embrace ancient Egyptian culture as reimagined, for instance, in Freemasonry, the arts and entertainment. Intrigued by the way Greek and Roman writers described ancient Egyptians – to Herodotus, they were 'Ethiopian', with dark skin and tightly curled hair – eighteenth- and early nineteenth-century scholars looked to Egyptian art for clues, based on the antiquities that had started to arrive in Europe in ever greater numbers. But they also, increasingly, looked to the bodies of the ancient Egyptians themselves, since the distinctive practice of mummification made these corpses perfect subjects for the new medical men of the era.

Because Western thought had long recognized Egypt as such an important ancient culture, polarized arguments have tried to claim it as both an African/black and a Caucasian/white civilization. Rupert Murdoch is not alone in his ideas. Most public considerations of this topic miss the key points that this chapter will consider, however: first, how ideas about race have been invented and exploited since the eighteenth century; and second, how the traumas of the transatlantic slave trade and colonization helped make ancient Egypt an important touchstone of identity among African diasporas and in several African countries. The chapter opens by considering how race science influenced the study of mummies and the development of Egyptology, which will help us understand how ancient Egypt became a symbol of both pride and prejudice, from the American abolitionist movement to Pan-Africanism. Ancient Egypt has been a source of inspiration for cultural movements like the Harlem Renaissance, which saw artists and literary figures evoke Egypt as a lost African homeland. In post-independence Senegal, ancient Egypt represented achievements with which all Africans could identify, or so argued the Senegalese academic Cheikh Anta Diop, whose work inspired an interpretation known as Afrocentrism that has been especially influential in the United States. Contemporary artists continue to use references to ancient Egypt as a way to confront themes of racial prejudice, Eurocentrism and the dark side of the Enlightenment, with its legacies of colonialism and the slave trade. It appears that Rupert Murdoch and Rihanna have ideas about ancient Egypt with longer and deeper roots than they may realize. But the reaction, interest or admiration their verbal or visual expressions generated indicates that this 'lost' civilization exposes our own sensitivities about more recently buried histories.

Racing the Egyptian mummy

The question 'What race were the ancient Egyptians?' assumes that 'race' is a fixed or useful concept: its answer often depends on who is asking it, and why. To understand how ancient Egypt became so entwined with this question, we have to return once again to eighteenth-century Europe, where the notion of 'race' was first formulated.[1] In the past fifty years biological and social scientists have abandoned race as a category, because the simple physical characteristics it relies on – skin colour, hair type, face shape and so on – do not map on to the kinds of genetic data, such as DNA, that modern techniques enable. The relationship between phenotype (external appearance) and a cline or cluster of genetic traits proves to be highly variable. Whether people identify themselves or others with a certain race profile depends on external appearance as well as social assumptions or expectations. Genetic data can be made to fit these (using DNA evidence to identify someone as Caucasian or East Asian, for instance) but also shows the tremendous variety of human populations, thanks to thousands of years of global migration – including more recent forced movements, such as slavery.

It was contact with other peoples as a result of European expansionism that encouraged eighteenth-century scholars such as Carl Linnaeus, in Sweden, and Petrus Camper, based in Amsterdam, to formulate the first classification systems for human racial difference. Camper measured skulls collected by travellers or derived from anatomical dissections, often using the bodies of criminals. He developed a system of representing heads in profile to show the angles between forehead, nose and jaw, which were meant to indicate the difference between 'European' and 'Ethiopian' or African types in particular.[2] Camper followed a common practice at the time, in comparing the profiles of human remains to the profiles of admired Classical statues such as the Apollo Belvedere in the Vatican. Assuming that the ancient Greeks had attained the pinnacle of realism in art, and that the Greeks were 'European', anatomists like Camper saw no difficulty in arranging the profiles of statues and of skulls in hierarchical rows. The statues were the most beautiful and most European, with their straight-up-and-down profile, while skulls that had strong lower jaws or prominent foreheads yielded steeper angles and thus were not European – and not beautiful.

Camper's influential schema did not consider ancient Egyptian art, since what little was known about it in Europe at the time found it lacking in comparison to Greek art, as we saw earlier. Instead, other anatomists realized that unwrapping ancient Egyptian mummies offered a unique opportunity to study the 'race' of an ancient population quite literally in the flesh, something impossible for the ancient Greeks, who practised cremation. In the 1790s the German scholar Johann Friedrich Blumenbach unwrapped Egyptian mummies (some of them fakes sold to early travellers) to augment his research on human variety. It was Blumenbach who coined the term 'Caucasian', based on skulls he collected from the Caucasus mountains in Georgia – one of which he described as the most beautiful skull he had ever seen. In the early nineteenth century mummy unwrappings became something of a fad among learned societies and surgeons keen to position themselves as experts in the newly professionalized medical field. The supply of fresh cadavers for anatomical dissection was still restricted, and more mummies were available in Europe in the wake of the Napoleonic expedition (and the end of the ensuing wars). Unwrapping a mummy killed several birds with one stone, so to speak. By the 1820s it was taken for granted that the head of an unwrapped mummy would be measured to determine its racial identity, using the methods Camper had devised and French zoologist Georges Cuvier had further developed. Thus the British-Italian surgeon Augustus Bozzi Granville confidently announced to the Royal Society in London that a female mummy he unwrapped was Caucasian. Granville noted that Cuvier also considered the ancient Egyptians to be a Caucasian population, while Blumenbach thought them closer to the Ethiopian race – later known as 'Negroid'.[3]

If learned men and medical specialists at first wished to classify human difference as an exercise in itself, pursuing a new form of knowledge in the Enlightenment spirit, it was nonetheless the case that the idea of racial difference soon became an instrument for racial prejudice. In 1830s Philadelphia, physician Samuel Morton made his own forays into race classification, using hundreds of skulls. His collection included the skulls of Native American peoples and skulls from ancient Egyptian mummies, the latter supplied from Egypt by the British-born American consul there, George Robbins Gliddon. Using lead shot, Morton measured the volume of skulls he had assigned to different races, and from this he suggested that different skull sizes implied different brain sizes, hence (he assumed) variations in mental capacity. Caucasians were the most intelligent race, while Native Americans were only just above Africans and Aboriginal Australians, who occupied the bottom of his ranking.[4] Morton (like Granville) determined that the ancient Egyptians were Caucasian, which rather conveniently fitted mainstream reasoning that Egypt was a great civilization and therefore a white one. Morton also proposed that the differences between human 'races' were so significant that humans were not one species but several, a theory known as polygenesis, 'many origins'. This seems preposterous now, but it was taken very seriously around the mid-nineteenth century, when the African slave trade was still active in the South Atlantic and the cotton and tobacco economies of the southern United States relied on slave labour. Morton's work

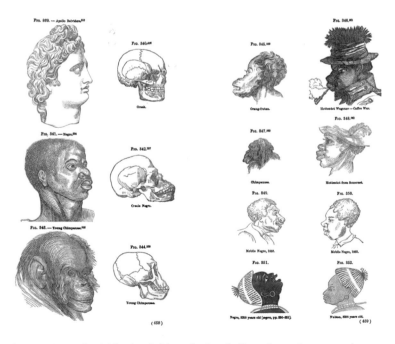

A comparison of racial (and racist) 'types', using skulls, sculpture, humans and animals, from Josiah Nott and George Gliddon, *Types of Mankind* (1854).

became influential among proponents of slavery, such as South Carolina Senator John Calhoun, who argued that all great societies, including ancient Egypt, consisted of an elite who owned slaves as a 'positive good' for everyone involved; besides which, the theory of polygenesis argued that enslaved races were from a different species, not true *Homo sapiens*. Recreating ancient Egypt as a white civilization that owned black slaves, just like the American South, seemed to account for differences among ancient Egyptian skulls and in ancient Egyptian art, which was increasingly acknowledged as representing a range of skin tones, hair textures and physiognomies.

After Morton's death, George Gliddon (his supplier of skulls from Egypt) collaborated with Alabama physician and plantation – hence, slave – owner Josiah Nott to produce a mammoth volume dedicated to his memory, called *Types of Mankind*.[5] First published in 1854, *Types of Mankind* proved so popular that it was reprinted eight times before the decade's end. In a chapter devoted to Egypt, Nott and Gliddon echoed the visualization methods of Camper's work by comparing the Egyptian skulls Morton had studied to hand-drawn copies of Egyptian wall paintings and reliefs in the works of early Egyptologists like Champollion. Some of these depicted captured soldiers or subservient traders with black African features, using a visual rhetoric that proclaimed the supremacy of Egypt over the known world. Nott and Gliddon had to admit, as Morton had, that the original 'Nilotic stock' of the ancient Egyptians was no longer 'pure' after around 2000 BC – but it was absolutely not 'Negroid', they argued, with 'Negro types' in Egypt strictly limited to the enslaved stratum of society. No mingling allowed. In mid-nineteenth-century America, anxieties about miscegenation were rooted in contemporaneous realities: the sexual exploitation of black slaves by their white masters was endemic.

Abhorrent theories like Nott and Gliddon's retreated somewhat, with the end of plantation slavery in the American Civil War and the rejection of polygenesis once Darwin's theory of evolution gained acceptance. But the assumptions at their core – that Caucasians are the most intelligent race, that Africans had no 'great' civilization – have never entirely gone away, living on in the invective of white supremacy and, of course, in cultural memory. Moreover, other forms of race science were fundamental in the development of entire scientific disciplines in the late nineteenth century, and not just biological sciences, but anthropology and archaeology as well. In the wake of Darwin, the idea that whole civilizations, as well as different human populations, were part of an ongoing evolutionary process suffused the thinking of many of the 'founding fathers' of these disciplines; and it still slips unnoticed into our own thinking any time we use a word such as 'primitive' or 'backwards' to describe another culture. One of the most influential figures in Egyptian archaeology, Flinders Petrie, was typical of his day in that his interpretations of the ancient past were steeped in ideas about race. In his studies of Egyptian prehistory, which was then a new field, Petrie theorized that a separate group of people from the north, termed the Dynastic Race, moved into the Nile Valley, intermarried with indigenous groups from the south, and thus catalysed the technological advancement that created 'civilization'. Petrie's theory offered a positive outcome to racial mixing, unlike the vitriol of Nott and Gliddon, but it is nonetheless a theory based on false premises – 'race' as a meaningful category, and 'northern' races as superior. In an echo of Gliddon, Petrie saved skulls he excavated in Egypt to send to his friend (and Darwin's cousin) Francis Galton, who ran an institute for the study of eugenics at University College London.[6] Petrie also compiled photographs of Egyptian art to identify and categorize different 'races' in antiquity.

Race science was built into the study of ancient Egypt from the start, from its mummies to its works of art, which approaches like Petrie's viewed as if they were representations of observed reality. Well into the twentieth century mummy unwrappings invariably commented on features that might indicate the body's race, and the heads and skulls of ancient Egyptian bodies were posed in profile, using the powerful trope instituted by Camper and further developed in nineteenth-century anthropometric recording techniques, for instance on ethnographic expeditions and in criminology. In 1925 the head of king Tutankhamun, detached from his body to help remove the gold mask, was propped on a wooden plank to take profile photographs, for instance. Today, the technology of CT-scans and three-dimensional imaging allows similar investigations to take place without physically unwrapping the body, or by revisiting bodies like Tutankhamun's. In 2005 CT-scans of the king's head were given to three separate teams in the United States, France and Egypt to allow them to reconstruct his appearance.[7] Only the French team were told whose body it was and it was their reconstruction – cappuccino-coloured skin, slender nose, nice eyeliner – that was splashed across the press. Some commentators saw it as not African enough; a few noticed how different it looked to the less visually arresting reconstructions by the other two teams, who did not know the scans were from the body of the famous pharaoh.

Reconstructions of ancient Egyptian bodies always raise debates around race: for all that such reconstructions appear irrefutable, they involve a degree of interpretation and estimation, especially for those features, such as nose contours, lip size and shape, and skin colour, most often taken as physical markers of race. Reading 'race' from Egyptian mummies is problematic for many reasons. In any case, the fact that mummification was the preserve of such a small elite means that mummies can only provide limited evidence about the ancient population as a whole – and even within that restricted data set there is tremendous diversity, as we should expect. Rather than ask what 'race' the ancient Egyptians were, perhaps the more interesting question to ask is what the racial identities attributed to ancient Egypt allow different people to remember in different ways.

Ancient rivers run deep

During the nineteenth century America looked to the civilizations of Greece, Rome and Egypt to find the oldest historical models on which to base its experimental form of nationhood. Hence the number of American cities named after Greek, Roman and Egyptian sites, from Athens, Ohio, to Memphis, Tennessee.[8] Egypt's great age and endurance lent gravity to newly founded settlements. Ancient Egypt was not too alien or exotic in this context, nor did it have to be seen, as *Types of Mankind* had it, as a civilization built on slavery. In fact, Egypt had a double meaning as the place where freedom from slavery could be gained, since the Bible recounted the exodus of Hebrew slaves from their years of imprisonment there. As the African American spiritual 'Go down, Moses' recalled:

> Go down, Moses
> Way down in Egypt Land.
> Tell old Pharaoh,
> Let my people go.

Ancient Egypt could thus be a source of identification and pride among both African Americans and white anti-slavery activists. But because of its dual associations – as a great civilization as well as an oppressive one, as a place of freedom as well as enslavement, as a place that was African as well as Middle Eastern or Mediterranean – ancient Egypt proved to be an unstable concept. That is, it made for a powerful symbol in a range of contexts, but its symbolic effectiveness stood on shaky ground. Ancient Greece seemed like a solid idea in comparison, and remains so today, not because our ideas about ancient Greece are any more 'accurate' than our ideas about ancient Egypt, but because they come with less (or different) cultural baggage attached.

African Americans living with the reality of slavery and its aftermaths were sensitive to these two Egypts: the land of slavery and the land of freedom. Sojourner Truth, herself a freed slave who helped others make the journey north, declared that she had left 'Egypt' behind her, while the African American abolitionists Henry Highland Garnet and Frederick Douglass (both also born into slavery) saw Egypt in a positive light, believing it to have been founded by the biblical Ham, son of Abraham, conventionally identified as black. The African American physician and historian Martin Robison Delany held a similar view of Egypt and advocated that his fellow black Americans – men only, of course – should embrace Freemasonry, which had a tradition of black lodges in America going back to the eighteenth century.[9] Long after the Civil War ended, African Americans faced deep prejudice and injustice, not only in southern states, where the lynching of black men was a violent expression of white prejudice into the 1960s, but in the north, where economic hardships, restricted opportunities and de facto segregation blighted day-to-day life for many blacks. Having social institutions (a Freemasons' lodge, a church) and cultural memories (ancient Egypt, independent Ethiopia) that embraced an African identity was a way to foster cohesion and pride in the face of a dominant, Eurocentric society.

Nor was identification with an African past (and present) only a concern in the United States. By the turn of the twentieth century African diasporas around the world, and especially in the former slave-owning countries of the West Indies and South America, sought solidarity with each other and with parts of Africa exploited by imperialism after the 1884 Berlin Conference of European powers set off the so-called 'scramble for Africa'. In 1900 the first Pan-African Conference met in London, bringing together delegates from the USA, Britain, the Caribbean and Ethiopia, which was one of only two self-governing nations in Africa at the time (the other was Liberia). The delegates petitioned for reforms that would restore dignity to colonies in Africa, concerns that were captured in a resounding address by delegate W.E.B. Du Bois, a leading African American intellectual. Although an international Pan-African meeting would not be held again until after the First World War, the phrase and the concept of Pan-Africanism were firmly lodged in cultural consciousness, and Egypt and Ethiopia were often held up as admired examples of African accomplishments. As Du Bois wrote in his classic *The Souls of Black Folk*, published in 1903, 'The shadow of a mighty Negro past flits through the tale of Ethiopia the Shadowy and of Egypt the Sphinx.'[10] If all Africans and people of African descent could unite through African-ness, they could more effectively organize and improve their conditions at home. Membership of any large, disparate group – like a nation – depends on imagining a shared sense of purpose, identity and origin. Ancient Egypt readily offered a symbol for Pan-Africanism, arguably all the more potent because it had been misappropriated by whites.

In the United States artists, writers and performers picked up on Pan-African ideals as they sought ways to give a voice, or a

Meta Warrick Fuller, *Ethiopia Awakening*, 1914, bronze sculpture.

vision, to African American experiences. In the 1920s and 1930s a loose collection of cultural figures became known as the Harlem Renaissance, named after a New York City neighbourhood, although the movement was in fact widespread.[11] Several of these artists and writers held up the achievements of ancient Egypt as a model for contemporary African Americans. The Harlem Renaissance was a Modernist movement, with many links to artists and

Lois Mailou Jones, *The Ascent of Ethiopia*, oil on canvas, 1932.

writers in Europe who were also, in their own ways, looking to Africa and ancient civilizations for inspiration.

Aaron Douglas, Meta Warrick Fuller and Lois Mailou Jones were three Harlem Renaissance artists who used ancient Egyptian motifs in their work. Warrick Fuller, a friend of Du Bois and protégée of Auguste Rodin, exhibited a bronze known as *Ethiopia* or *Ethiopia Awakening* at The Armory in New York in 1921.[12] The exhibition, called 'America's Making', emphasized America's 'melting-pot' pluralism, and Du Bois helped design the section that would represent the heritage and contributions of African Americans. In a booth adorned with the Great Pyramid and sphinx at Giza, *Ethiopia* represented the emancipation not only of slaves in America, but of the entire 'Negro race', in the terms of the day. Warrick Fuller's statue shows an African woman in the *nemes*-headscarf of an Egyptian pharaoh, emerging into life from the mummy wrappings that bind her legs. The choice of Ethiopia, rather than Egypt, as the name of the work reflects the close relationship between the two as mythic ideals of Africa, both with ancient histories ('Ethiopia' was what Greek and Roman writers termed sub-Saharan Africa) and both with impressive associations. As a Christian country, Ethiopia complemented the pagan gods of ancient Egypt, and in the 1920s Ethiopia also held an appeal because of its imperial identity: its regent at the time was Ras Tafari, crowned emperor in 1930 as Haile Selassie, 'The Power of the Trinity'.

Lois Mailou Jones similarly used Ethiopia, rather than Egypt, in the title of her Egyptian-themed *The Ascent of Ethiopia*, an oil painting from 1932.[13] The profile head and shoulders of a dark-skinned Egyptian queen or goddess dominate the lower right of the canvas, while a celestial body – sun, moon and star at once – beams from top left onto figures of Africans rising past the pyramids and climbing steps towards skyscrapers above the queen's head. Around the illuminated towers, concentric circles representing art, music and drama capture the spirit of the Harlem Renaissance. Jones acknowledged her debt to Meta Warrick Fuller: 'Ethiopia' in her painting's name consciously echoed Warrick Fuller's sculpture, although it was recognizably ancient Egypt that provided the visual theme in both works.

Ancient Egypt was one of many lost homelands denied to the descendants of American slavery by the cruel circumstances under which their ancestors reached the New World, and for all that Egypt could offer inspiration for the future, it was also a place of mournful memory. The best-known poet and writer of the Harlem Renaissance was Langston Hughes, whose 1920 poem 'The Negro Speaks of Rivers' evokes these lost homelands, from the lands of the Bible, through Africa, to the United States. In the poem's phrase, 'rivers ancient as the world' have been part of black ('Negro') history: the Euphrates in Iraq, the Congo in West Africa, the Mississippi that joins the American North and South, and of course the Nile with its pyramids built by the poem's nameless narrator. With this evocative imagery, Hughes places black experience at the heart of Western civilization. It cannot be overlooked or excised – and like a river, it has a powerful current and runs long and deep.

The Black Land

Egypt as an African homeland spoke to African Americans in the decades after the abolition of slavery in the United States, especially in the 'jazz age' of the 1920s, when the discovery of Tutankhamun's tomb added to the lustre and lure of ancient Egyptian civilization. After the upheavals of the Second World War, when African countries began to gain independence from colonial powers like France and Britain, they too looked to the continent's history to forge new identities. The former Rhodesia, for instance, took its new name from the archaeological site of Great Zimbabwe, while former French colonies, like Senegal, took inspiration from *Négritude*, a Francophone intellectual movement with origins in the 1920s, promoting black accomplishments and opposing colonialism. Like the Harlem Renaissance, *Négritude* was indebted to Pan-African ideas, but different movements and their adherents formulated and used these ideas in distinctive ways, especially in the post-war political climate.

In the 1950s and 1960s a respected physicist, historian and sometime politician in Senegal, Cheikh Anta Diop, published several influential works emphasizing the cultural unity of Africa. Diop's approach was resolutely Pan-African: he saw all indigenous Africans as a homogeneous race with social, political and linguistic traits that remained fixed over millennia, as far back as ancient Egypt. Coming of age as he did in the closing decades of French colonialism – and having himself studied in France – seems to have drawn Diop towards a racialized way of thinking, as if the problems facing Senegal and other emerging African nations were literally black and white. Unlike the *Négritude* movement, which celebrated contemporary African cultural expressions, and in which Senegal's first president Leopold Senghor was a leading figure, the approach taken by Diop stressed deep-rooted historical factors and innate racial traits that made Africans more enlightened, more cultivated and fundamentally different than the Europeans who had oppressed and exploited them for so long. Diop sometimes used evidence that was selective, or tenuous, to make his arguments, for instance using phonetic similarities between unrelated languages like Wolof and ancient Egyptian to conclude that Senegalese people descended from ancient Egyptians who had migrated to West Africa.[14] Bolstered by Diop's high personal profile, especially after he entered politics, his views reached a wide audience. They struck a chord with some Senegalese, as they continue to do today. Origin myths based on migration feature in several West African countries, some perhaps ways of remembering – or rather, forgetting – the displacements forced on West and Central Africans by the trans-atlantic slave trade. That ancient Egyptians had once settled along the Senegal river was a less painful cultural memory to incorporate into the new nation's consciousness.

In 1974 two of Diop's earlier books were combined to produce an English translation, *The African Origin of Civilization: Myth or Reality.* Its publication extended the influence of Diop's work to the Anglophone world and especially the United States, where his ideas chimed with a range of black power movements that had emerged from the civil rights movement. As we saw earlier in this chapter, African Americans already had a long history of identifying with ancient Egypt, though this was by no means straightforward or universal. Still, several u.s.-based historians of African descent had written revisionist accounts of ancient Egypt's contribution to world history, for instance asserting that ancient Egyptians were the originators of ancient Greek philosophy or, in echoes of Diop, that ancient Egyptians and other black Africans had sailed to the new world before Columbus. The publication of *The African Origin of Civilization* helped coalesce these varied trends into a school of thought known as Afrocentrism. In the 1980s the author and activist Molefi Kete Asante articulated the Afrocentric project as an overdue shift from Eurocentric views of history and civilization.[15] Asante identified the ancient Egyptians as black and promoted the use of the ancient word 'Kemet', meaning 'the black land', for the ancient Egyptian civilization. Blackness mattered: it was a form of identity with which African Americans were confronted every day, and extending black identity through time and space offered a way to prioritize African contributions that had been ignored, overlooked or written out of history altogether.

Afrocentrism proved to be a broad school of thought, encompassing a range of ideas and approaches. Although it has its own conferences, university programmes and published outputs, Afrocentrism is more than an academic theory or methodology. It has informed education provision in many schools and museums, for instance, where staff cite its value in promoting a sense of personal pride and achievement among disadvantaged pupils with African American or other non-white backgrounds. At one extreme, some Afrocentric ideas drift into ideology, reiterating essentialist, invidious and, in some cases, anti-Semitic notions of race that mirror, rather than challenge, racist ideologies like white supremacism. But as a way to draw much-needed attention to the rich histories of the African continent, and to the reasons why these histories have not been told, Afrocentrism has also proved to be a powerful and positive voice, with ancient Egypt one of the key platforms for articulating its themes.

Afrocentrism garnered national attention in the United States in 1987 with the publication of the first volume of (white) historian Martin Bernal's *Black Athena: The Afroasiatic Roots of Classical Civilization*.[16] The grandson of the British Egyptologist Alan Gardiner, who had played a small role in the initial work on Tutankhamun's tomb, Bernal was a specialist in Chinese history who initially undertook the research for *Black Athena* as a sideline. The book was an unapologetically academic tome that eventually ran to three volumes, but it had a passionate – some would say, polemical – thesis at its heart. Bernal started from the premise that European scholarship on ancient Greek civilization had its roots in the eighteenth-century Enlightenment and its flowering in the racialized atmosphere of the nineteenth and early twentieth centuries. This is now not as controversial a premise perhaps (it should sound familiar from this book), but at the time studies of classical antiquity had done little to question explicitly what impact this might have had on the formation of the discipline. Bernal argued that bias, especially in German-speaking academia, had led earlier scholars to downplay significant connections and influences that flowed both from the ancient Semitic-speaking world of southwest Asia (the Levant, Syria, Iraq and southeastern Turkey) and from ancient Egypt to early Greek civilization, which, after all, was made up of seafaring societies that traded all around the eastern Mediterranean and beyond. It was his publisher, Bernal later stated, that encouraged the evocative book title *Black Athena*, which reduced his complex arguments to a re-branding of classical Greece – that cherished font of European civilization – as 'black'.

Bernal did not identify himself as Afrocentrist, but some Afrocentric scholars and activists embraced him as one of their own. Here was an establishment figure, and a white academic at that, garnering attention and lending support to ideas that seemed broadly similar, although the fact that it took a white scholar's work to bring Afrocentrism to mainstream attention speaks volumes. Bernal rejected racial classification on the same grounds any conventional Egyptologist would do today, namely that 'race' is a historical and cultural construct, not a biological reality. As reaction to *Black Athena* proved, though, that was not the point: race matters where the study of ancient Egypt was concerned because race matters in our own society.

Classicists, archaeologists and Egyptologists identified many holes in the evidence Bernal used and pointed out that his general idea about cross-cultural exchanges in the ancient Mediterranean was much more widely accepted than he implied. There had been no conspiracy to downgrade African and Middle Eastern contributions to the specific cultural forms that developed on the Greek mainland, the islands and around the Black Sea. But it is true that over the eighteenth and nineteenth centuries Europe's own myth-making about its origins had driven a wedge between the northern and southern shores of the Mediterranean Sea, a division amplified by the nation-building efforts of Greece and other countries, including Germany. No form of knowledge is pure and infallible, untainted by the circumstances in which it is produced. That holds for classical or Egyptological scholarship produced in Fascist Germany as much as it does for Afrocentric scholarship produced in riot-torn 1990s Los Angeles. Even among the most diligent academics, what constitutes knowledge, evidence and sound argumentation can take many forms, and as soon as we expand these questions of epistemology – the science of knowledge – beyond academia, it is clear that one group's consensus is another's glaring fallacy. Where the concept of cultural memory can help is by reminding us that such controversies usually signal that other issues are at stake. Whether ancient Egypt was black or white, African or European, impinges on the cultural memory of 'our' lost civilization – and depends on who that 'our' includes.

From the 1980s to the present day the American artist Fred Wilson has created a number of museum interventions and works of art that draw attention to suppressed cultural memories, such as American slavery (the artist is himself of African descent). For the 1992 Cairo Biennale, Wilson looked to ancient Egypt and its legacies for an installation he entitled *Re:Claiming Egypt*. He combined casts and other replicas of ancient Egyptian art with everyday objects like souvenirs, books and clothing, all of which presented ancient Egypt as a black African culture. Wilson was not necessarily promoting an Afrocentric view of ancient Egyptian culture, but rather drawing attention to the debate and the reasons behind it, such as the black/white dichotomy inherited from nineteenth-century race science. In one work, *Grey Area*, he lined up five plaster casts of the bust of Nefertiti (she of Rihanna's side tattoo), which he had painted in shades ranging from black to white. For another version of the piece (*Grey Area, Brown Version*), now in the Brooklyn Museum of Art, Wilson used shades of 'skin' tone to paint the plaster busts instead, running like a cosmetic foundation chart from pale ivory to dark chocolate.

By usurping this iconic artwork, Wilson confronts viewers with the assumptions that each of us makes about skin colour, identity and heritage – while his title, *Grey Area*, seems to admit that

Fred Wilson, *Grey Area (Black Version),* painted plaster, 1993.

uncertainty and unknowability are built into our encounter with the ancient past. That past is only available to us through its material remains and our own imaginations, with the caveat that how we imagine it may depend on who we are. More interesting than arguing for a right or a wrong way to visualize ancient Egypt is reflecting on what different visualizations say about the individuals and societies that produce them, whether that is Rupert Murdoch and his 'white' Egyptians, or the Egyptian football players who made 'walk like an Egyptian' arm gestures during their 2008 African Cup of Nations victory in Ghana – national pride expressed within an African sporting context.[17] Ideas of heritage have become intrinsically tied up with what is often called the politics of recognition or, disparagingly, identity politics. Yet public assertions of European mastery over Egypt, such as obelisks erected in capital cities, are rarely critiqued for accuracy or fairness, the way that African and diaspora identifications with ancient Egypt have been in mainstream Western media. Moreover, amid the competing claims to an ancient Egypt that is white or black, European or African, what is often overlooked, dismissed or ignored is the way that modern Egyptians have sought their own identity in ancient Egypt in the course of the nineteenth, twentieth and now twenty-first centuries.

EIGHT

Counting the
Years

The painted plaster bust of queen Nefertiti has become a fluid symbol, signifying 'ancient Egypt' in contexts from body art to the art gallery – and recently in the art of protest, too. In September 2012 the Egyptian street artist El Zeft applied a new sticker to the wall of protest graffiti along Mohammed Mahmoud Street in downtown Cairo. The street gives out onto Tahrir Square, site of the January and February 2011 demonstrations that ended the thirty-year rule of President Hosni Mubarak. On Mohammed Mahmoud Street and elsewhere in the city graffiti mocked Mubarak and the Egyptian military, vented frustration as the aims of the revolution were stymied by the army's continued sway, and commemorated men and women killed during the protests.[1] The sticker El Zeft applied to the wall that September, nearly two years after the Tahrir occupation, showed Nefertiti in her distinctive flat-topped crown, eyes straight on under lowered brows – and a gas mask covering her lower face. In a Facebook post announcing the new work, the artist described it as a tribute to the women who had played such an important part in the revolution. Nefertiti represented Egyptian women, ancient and modern, girded for protest with her tear gas protection, although the mask covering the queen's mouth could also be seen as a muzzle or stifling gag. Presumably because the ancient bust the sticker mimics was so instantly recognizable around the world, versions of El Zeft's artwork were taken up by protesters not only in Cairo but in Amman,

El Zeft's sticker-graffito *Nefertiti in a Gas Mask*, Cairo, 2012.

Berlin and Seoul. Amnesty International used the image several times in its protests against state suppression of the Egyptian revolution, and it also appeared in international demonstrations against the sexual harassment and assaults that women protesters and journalists faced during the uprising. If Nefertiti looks angry, with her confrontational gaze, she has plenty of reasons to be.

Icons of ancient Egypt – Nefertiti and Tutankhamun, the pyramids and the sphinx – have long been incorporated into contemporary Egyptian life, from postage stamps and currency notes to revolutionary graffiti like El Zeft's. But how these icons resonate in Egypt differs in some ways from the associations they have outside the Middle East. For a start, Egypt has many other cultural phenomena and influences on which to draw, not least its rich heritage under the Umayyad Caliphate and in the Fatimid era; the Ottoman period represented by Mohamed Ali and his successors; and twentieth-century accomplishments as the country gained its independence and became a key (if sometimes controversial) player in northeast African and Middle Eastern geopolitics. To expect today's Egyptians to identify only with the ancient past would be akin to thinking everyone in Britain should be fervently and exclusively interested in Stonehenge or the Avebury ring. Some people in Britain are interested in stone circles, perhaps because they live near them, or study them, or self-identify as pagans and see these monuments as sacred sites. However, most people in Britain pay little attention to stone circles on a day-to-day basis, although they would no doubt recognize an image of Stonehenge and express alarm or outrage if it were threatened with destruction, so deeply have these monoliths become part of the nation's cultural memory since the eighteenth century, when the antiquarian William Stukeley helped to popularize them.

In Egypt how modern citizens might think about and experience the ancient past is made more complex by the experience of colonialism. Like many other colonized countries whose archaeological remains attracted Western attention, Egypt has found itself in the peculiar position of having its own past re-classified, represented and often simply just removed by foreigners. The country's Ottoman governors also used Egyptian antiquities for diplomatic exchanges with Western powers, in a gifting network that helped Mohamed Ali and the later khedives augment their own prestige while securing what they saw as benefits for Egypt's modernization and infrastructure. Mohamed Ali gave obelisks to Britain and France (now on the Thames Embankment and the Place de la Concorde); Said *pasha* showered the future King Edward vii, while he was Prince of Wales, with coffins and other antiquities during his 1862 tour of Egypt; and the Austro-Hungarian emperor Franz Josef i was rewarded for his visit to the opening of the Suez Canal with three temple columns, which now help hold up the Egyptian galleries in Vienna's Kunsthistorisches Museum. Large quantities of ancient Egyptian objects left Egypt for Western museums under the division of finds that the French-run antiquities service operated for almost a century, which was meant to recompense foreign archaeologists for the excavations they undertook in Egypt, with government permission. Today some Egyptians describe a sense of displacement when they visit museums in Europe or North America and see so many Egyptian antiquities on display: is this a good thing, promoting Egyptian culture around the world? Or is it a reminder of how Egypt's past has been appropriated for so many other purposes, rather than entrusted to Egyptian hands?

This chapter considers just some of the ways in which modern Egyptians have engaged with archaeology and ancient Egyptian culture. First, it looks at the contributions Egyptians made to excavations up and down the country – and at the barriers that faced Egyptians who wanted to study Egyptology in the nineteenth and early twentieth centuries. The credit given to Western archaeologists for their discoveries ignores the crucial roles that Egyptians played on many levels in excavations, and continue to today. Second, when Egypt gained a limited independence from Britain in 1922, it was amid a cultural movement known as Pharaonism, which – like the Harlem Renaissance or *Négritude* – looked to the past to cultivate pride in the present and hope for the future. In the wake of the 1952 revolution, moves towards decolonization and Pan-Arab unity ultimately gave way to the Camp David peace agreement and free-market reforms that further allied Egypt to the United States, a shifting geopolitics that complicated even more the relationship between Egypt's citizens, its state and the use of the ancient past. Like El Zeft, creator of the Nefertiti graffito, some Egyptian contemporary artists have turned to motifs from ancient Egypt to comment on the country's modern troubles, suggesting that degrees of connection to – or disconnection from – Egypt's ancient heritage not only characterize aspects of Egyptian self-identity today, but help to draw attention to issues within Egypt that should be of global concern.

Excavating Egypt

Too many books, classes and documentaries about the history of Egyptology start with what they call the 'discovery' or 'rediscovery' of Egypt by Europeans, as if Egypt were as devoid of human presence as the frontispiece to the Napoleonic *Description* imagined (for illustration, see Chapter Two). The choice of words implies that Europeans were finding something for the first time, or locating something they had lost. However, we have seen in this book that when, where and how Western culture remembered, or forgot about, ancient Egypt depended on many factors. Egypt was never lost, as the people who lived there knew perfectly well. Over the centuries Egyptians had their own ways of remembering and forgetting antiquity: turning temples into churches or mosque sites, recycling ancient stelae into buildings, or puzzling over pyramids and hieroglyphs, as al-Baghdadi and Ibn Wahshiya did in the Middle Ages. When Europeans began to travel to Egypt in the early nineteenth century and record its antiquities, they dismissed practices like recycling stones or building mosques and houses over temples as wilful destruction, proof that 'the Oriental' did not appreciate the ancient past in the way a 'civilized' European could. But seen from a different perspective, these practices constituted other ways of preserving antiquity, repurposing it in ways that suited the local population and that often acknowledged the ancient significance, for instance, by maintaining a site's religious use.

Besides which, an archaeological site only became an archaeological site once 'archaeology' itself existed: the word gained currency in the 1840s to distinguish emerging practices for studying and interpreting the past from earlier, antiquarian approaches. An 'antiquity' or an archaeological 'object' also had to be defined as such, first through the practice of archaeology and later through laws that defined certain things as 'antiquities' and changed who could own them and what could be done with them. Rather than see these as developments that were simply imported from Europe to Egypt, and that were inherently superior to what went before, it is both more accurate and more useful to see them as developments that took place within Egypt and as part of broader trends in land use, finance and diplomacy. In 1835 Mohamed Ali passed a declaration that no antiquities would leave the country and established his own museum, inspired by what his adviser, Rifa'a al-Tahtawi, had seen during his studies in France.[2] Al-Tahtawi was an imam, a scholarly translator and a prolific writer, who later authored textbooks for Egyptian schools that emphasized the accomplishments of ancient Egypt. Nonetheless, the American consul in Egypt, George Gliddon (co-author of the racist *Types of Mankind*), excoriated Mohamed Ali as a despot who was responsible for the wholesale destruction of Egyptian antiquities, echoing the widespread European belief that 'Orientals' were lazy, greedy and untrustworthy.[3] Mohamed Ali's ineffectiveness at controlling the export of antiquities was in part a function of the tremendous pressure from European interests competing with each other to form prestigious collections – and to create commercial opportunities for themselves in Egypt. Mohamed Ali's collection of antiquities also fell prey to diplomatic motives: his immediate successor, Abbas I (ruled 1848–54), gave part of it to the Ottoman Sultan Abd al-Aziz, and his son Said (1854–63) gifted the remainder to Archduke Maximilian of Austria.[4]

Despite giving away what was left of his father's collection, Said was ready to take up the challenge of keeping more of his country's antiquities in Egypt: in 1858 he established a Service des antiquités (antiquities service) in the ministry of public works, to coordinate archaeology in the country. He also re-established a museum, at Boulaq in Cairo, to house objects discovered by the new excavations.[5] Said hired the Egyptologist and one-time curator at the Louvre museum, Auguste Mariette, to direct the Service, and

Mariette spent the rest of his career in Egypt, in the employ first of Said, and then of Ismail (ruled 1863–79) and Tawfik (1879–82). In addition to organizing his own excavations and running the museum, Mariette began to license the work of other excavators, using a permit system. He also helped present the accomplishments of Egyptian archaeology abroad, for instance organizing the Egyptian pavilion at the 1867 Exposition universelle in Paris, which included antiquities lent by Egypt and displayed in a replica Egyptian temple.

In Mariette's day, able-bodied men, as well as women and children, were expected to contribute labour on government-sponsored projects (the Suez Canal was one notable example), facing financial penalties or corporal punishment if they refused. Expanded under Mohamed Ali, the *corvée* system was pervasive in the 1850s and 1860s, and it supplied much of the labour for archaeological clearance projects at this time, as well. The social memory of excavation in Egypt may thus include memories of hardship and exploitation, as the lyrics of labourers' work-songs of the time suggest.[6] By the 1880s the *corvée* was on the decline, since methods of year-round farming and paid employment proved more productive for the new, large-scale agricultural estates and factories. Archaeological labour followed this trend, which went hand-in-hand with the increasing specialization that excavation required. Archaeology had begun to present itself as a rational, scientific discipline requiring specific techniques, and archaeologists like Flinders Petrie (active in Egypt from the 1880s to the 1920s) and George Reisner (from the 1900s to the 1940s) gave some of their Egyptian staff limited training in fieldwork and recording methods. This was not because scholars like Petrie or Reisner wished to encourage Egyptians into the archaeology profession. Both men were typical in assuming that Egyptians lacked the intellectual capacity and logical reasoning such scientific work required. Training selected Egyptian staff in certain skills simply made for a more efficient dig, besides which, paying 'natives' was cheaper than hiring a student or junior academic from overseas.

In 1869 Khedive Ismail's reformist minister for education, Ali Mubarak, opened a School of Egyptology in Cairo, appointing the

German Egyptologist Heinrich Brugsch as its director.[7] It may have been only a small part of Mubarak's wide-scale reorganization of public education, but it was an important one in that Mubarak felt strongly that Egyptians should understand, and take pride in, their ancient past, which meant integrating Western scholarship into Egyptian education. One hope in setting up the School was that it would train Egyptian men to contribute to the work of the antiquities service, which was rapidly expanding – as was the Egyptian upper middle class, which had the Western-style education needed to follow Brugsch's curriculum in German and French. The new School attracted several excellent students from this milieu, including Ahmed Kamal, a near-contemporary of Petrie. When Kamal and the other students completed their training, however, they found it impossible to secure work as Egyptologists: Mariette refused to hire them in the Service and the School of Egyptology was closed just five years after it opened. Kamal spent several years teaching and translating German instead. Only when Mariette was dying, and the more liberal-minded Gaston Maspero, a French Egyptologist, was in line to replace him, did Kamal secure his first appointment in Egyptology, in the Boulaq Museum – although tellingly, it was not as a curator, but as a translator.[8]

Kamal took inspiration from Ali Mubarak and his old teacher Heinrich Brugsch to establish a training programme in Egyptology at the museum for his fellow Egyptians. Though it ran for only five years, several of Kamal's students went on to careers in the antiquities service. In the 1900s Kamal also lectured at the newly founded Egyptian (now Cairo) University and developed an Egyptology course for the Higher Teachers College. Well into the twentieth century, however, career opportunities for Egyptians in Egyptology and archaeology remained limited. Despite his copious publications, in both French and Arabic, and his knowledge of ancient and modern languages, Kamal was passed over for promotion within the antiquities service throughout his career, seeing younger European scholars appointed over him. For all the frustrations he himself faced, Kamal was an influence and inspiration for later generations of Egyptian Egyptologists, and an important contributor to the first, and most dramatic, discovery made under Mariette's successor, Maspero. High in the Deir el-Bahri cliffs at Luxor, Kamal – a Cairo-born sophisticate, with little experience outside the classroom – was about to come face-to-face with his rural, southern countrymen and with the mummies of ancient Egypt's most famous kings.

Mourning Egypt

Maspero took up the directorship of the Service in the spring of 1881, a tense time for the country. For several years Britain, France and Italy, whose banks held most of Egypt's national debt, had been managing the country's affairs from behind the scenes. Britain had forced Khedive Ismail out of office in 1879 (he abdicated in favour of his son Tawfik), and the European powers implemented severe funding cuts and increased tax collections, which hit the country's poor the hardest. The same upper middle-class milieu from which Ahmed Kamal originated had begun to chafe against European dominance of Egypt's affairs, and Ottoman sway as well. Most of the highest-ranking offices in the government and military were held by people of Turco-Circassian origin. Egyptian-born ministers such as Ali Mubarak, who was also a military officer, were the exception. In the late 1870s the Egyptian politician and army officer Ahmed Urabi emerged as leader of a popular rebellion that aimed to throw off European control and depose Tawfik – and in the summer of 1881 it looked like Urabi's supporters might succeed.[9]

In Qena, the province where Luxor was located, the governor (*mudir*) was an Urabi supporter, but he was also an official with a job to do. Taking up the Service directorship in the spring of 1881, Maspero identified an antiquities dealer named Ahmed Abd er-Rassul as a potential source of rare objects that had been trickling onto the market, objects that could come only from previously unknown royal burials of the 21st Dynasty. As a government official himself, Maspero submitted a request for the *mudir* of Qena, Daoud *pasha*, to arrest Abd er-Rassul and one of his brothers. The men were taken to the government offices in Qena and beaten in the presence of a local antiquities service inspector, trying to extract a confession about the unknown tombs, without success. The experience seems to have divided the Abd er-Rassul family, which lived in the village of Gurna on the West Bank of the Nile, among the ancient tombs. A third brother, Mohamed Abd er-Rassul, turned informant in July 1881 and Maspero immediately sent Ahmed Kamal and another museum employee, Emil Brugsch (younger brother of Heinrich), to Luxor to investigate. Abd er-Rassul led Kamal and Brugsch to an opening concealed in the cliff face between the village and the site known as Deir el-Bahri. A narrow, twisting corridor led more than 60 metres into the rock, lined with coffins, mummies, boxes of *shabti*-figures and vessels. Not only did this cleverly hidden tomb contain the burials of the high priests who ruled as kings in the Third Intermediate Period, but it contained the reburials of some of the most famous rulers of the New Kingdom, including Ramses II and his father Seti I. The priests of Amun had rewrapped and reburied these kings in secret after their tombs in the Valley of the Kings were violated, almost five hundred years after their deaths in some cases. Inscriptions on the new shrouds and recycled coffins detailed what the priests had done: these mummies were sacred objects, after all, and rewrapping and moving them was an act of reverence.[10]

Kamal and Brugsch could scarcely believe it. Maspero later recalled Brugsch telling him that it was like being in a dream. With the location of the tomb no longer the Abd er-Rassul family secret, however, Brugsch, Kamal and their colleague Tadros Moutafian had to snap out of the dream and act quickly to clear the tomb and move its contents to Cairo. Within 48 hours they had organized the clearance of the entire team, supervised by an experienced *reis* (in the context of archaeology, a chief of works or foreman). Daoud *pasha*, the *mudir*, conscripted three hundred local men to carry the coffins and crated antiquities (some 6,000 objects in total) down the cliffs and more than 5 miles across the valley to the Nile, in the ferocious summer heat. The overland journey took eight hours, with some of the coffins and their resin-rich contents so heavy that it needed a dozen men to lift them. At the river, the Boulaq Museum's steamboat arrived to carry the cargo to Cairo, where the museum would be the new resting place of these pharaohs and their families. As the boat made its way downstream,

Maspero wrote, women came to the shore to wail like mourners at a funeral.

Conventional histories of Egyptology often repeat Maspero's account as if these mourning women had stepped out of the funeral processions on ancient Egyptian tomb walls, and Maspero himself might have made the same connection, looking for 'survivals' of ancient culture among Egyptian peasants in the nineteenth century. This was a common assumption, that peasant life was largely unchanged since ancient times, but it was (and remains) a mistaken one. Egypt's peasants were as much a part of 1881 as Maspero and Kamal, their lives shaped by colonial capitalism's shift towards large-scale agricultural estates and monopolist industries, and by acts of rebellion that would come to a head in 1882, when the British invaded by land and sea to crush Urabi's challenge. Maspero seemed to think the weeping women were mourning the ancient dead, the 'freight of kings' the steamboat carried.[11] But what if they were mourning some other loss instead? Not least the forced removal of the mummies – and the self-determination (and source of income) they represented – from Qena province to the distant capital.

The mummies from the Deir el-Bahri cache were eventually unwrapped and put on display in Cairo. When the museum moved in 1902 to its new, specially designed building in Tahrir (then Ismailiya) Square, the royal corpses were one of the highlights for foreign tourists. At times the galleries of royal mummies have been closed to public view, notably for part of the 1920s and 1930s, when the mummies were moved to the (then unused) pharaonic-style mausoleum of nationalist hero Sa'ad Zaghloul, and in the 1980s, after President Anwar Sadat visited and expressed dismay at the undignified display of the dead.[12] Since the late 1980s, however, the so-called 'mummy rooms' have been reopened to visitors, with numbers restricted (and funds raised) by separate admission tickets. The rooms have been refitted with dimmer lighting and state-of-the-art vitrines, and the bared bodies are covered from neck to ankle by sheets in what is always characterized as a 'respectful' form of display. Whether the display of the dead in this way can ever be 'respectful' remains a point of debate, however, in Western museums and in Egypt as well. One outspoken Egyptian tour guide, Bassam el-Shammaa, launched his own campaign in 2013, calling for the royal mummies to be returned to the Valley of the Kings. He bases his argument in part on Islamic teachings, which say that burial is how one honours the dead: 'Shouldn't we hold our great kings in respect?', el-Shammaa has said in interviews. 'This should under no circumstances happen to our forefathers.'[13]

The pharaohs as forefathers of modern Egypt is one way in which Egyptian cultural memory links the country's present and its past, but not without ambivalence. The pharaoh can also be a figure of despotism, as he is in the Quran and the Bible: when Islamist military officers assassinated Anwar Sadat during a military parade in 1981, one of them is said to have shouted 'I have killed pharaoh!' Moreover, some of the tensions of the 1881 discovery have continued to echo down the decades, such as the frustrated anti-colonial ambitions of the Urabi movement; the link between archaeology, state power and Western intervention in Egypt's affairs; and the estrangement between urban elites in the north and the rural poor in the antiquities-rich south.

In 1969 director Shadi Abd al-Salam's film *al-Mumiya* (The Mummies) dramatized the Deir el-Bahri discovery with Ahmed

Engraving (probably based on a photograph) of visitors viewing the royal mummies in the Giza Palace antiquities museum, around 1890.

Kamal as one of the lead characters, whose foil is a character representing Mohamed Abd er-Rasul ('Wanis Harbat').[14] Known in English as 'The Night of Counting the Years', after an ancient Egyptian text intoned by the Maspero character in the film's opening scene, the film was only released in Egypt in 1975 after earning prizes in European festivals and praise from foreign critics, who admired its cinematic form. Western critics and academics, including Egyptologists, have tended to interpret the film as an unproblematic call for Egyptians to cherish their ancient heritage. Abd al-Salam himself spoke of the film as a story of two Egypts, the educated, progressive Egypt of the Cairene and Alexandrian elite and the uneducated, backwards Egypt of the rural south. With his *effendi* status, *tarboush* (or fez, worn by Ottoman civil servants), and state employment, Ahmed Kamal in the film (and arguably in life) represents the former. As a representative of the government, he ventures south to rescue antiquities and, in doing so, to rescue Egyptian peasants from their purported ignorance. Kamal, the film character, is spiritually enriched by his encounter with the 'authentic' Egyptian culture the rural poor represent, while the poor, like Wanis, benefit from recognizing the true significance of the antiquities they have been plundering – a significance that is predicated on the values of modern, rational, Western laws and science. Those Egyptian critics who praised *al-Mumiya* tried to reconcile its themes with the politics of the post-Nasser era, which were more ambivalent and less triumphalist about national identity following Israel's defeat of an Egyptian-led coalition in the 1967 war. The film could be read, for instance, as an account of how colonialism alienated Egyptians from their 'authentic' culture, but this relies on the nationalist idea that the ancient past is the most 'true' expression of an innate and inalienable Egyptian identity. There was, and is, a striking parallel between this nationalist view and Orientalist views of Egypt, which likewise place an idealized peasant in timeless connection to the past, as if modernity only happened elsewhere.

Egyptian nationalism had gathered pace between the 1882 British occupation that defeated Urabi (who was exiled to Sri Lanka for twenty years) and the limited independence Britain granted Egypt in 1922, after years of campaigning, resistance and an abortive revolution in 1919. As the new nation state found its bearings, its cultural and political leaders, most drawn from the upper middle classes, enlisted ancient Egyptian symbols to imagine a future for Egypt that could draw confidence from the country's past. *Al-firawniya* – interest in the pharaonic past, or Pharaonism – was a popular literary and artistic phenomenon in the 1920s. The real Ahmed Kamal lived just long enough, until August 1923, to witness the first independent election of an Egyptian parliament, and to follow news of the discovery of a new royal burial on the West Bank of Luxor: the tomb of Tutankhamun.

Reawakening Egypt

In the hopeful mood that accompanied Egyptian independence, the discovery of an intact burial in the Valley of the Kings could not have come at a better time for the country's new government, led by prime minister Sa'ad Zaghloul. Pharaonic motifs were already part of the nationalist iconography of Zaghloul's political party, the Wafd, and the 1919 revolution helped inspire a generation of artists and writers who would explore what it meant to be Egyptian by using imagery from ancient times. The painter Muhammad Nagi, who came from an elite Turco-Circassian family in Alexandria, studied fine art in Florence and with Claude Monet at Giverny, but Nagi also spent time at Luxor, copying tomb paintings on the West Bank. After the 1919 revolution he began a painting he called *Nahdat Misr*, the 'Reawakening of Egypt' or 'Revival of Egypt'. Finished by 1922, when it won a prize in Paris, the painting was chosen to decorate the parliament building inaugurated in Cairo in 1924.[15] It shows the goddess Isis in a chariot pulled by water buffalo, leading a procession of Egyptians in peasant dress: one man plays an *oud*, another holds an ancient bull statuette and women carry agricultural products. Children are naked, as in ancient Egyptian art, and a lush Nile Valley landscape extends along the background. As in Shadi Abd el-Salam's later film, these idealized Egyptian peasants symbolize the 'true' Egypt that can progress to modernity by looking to its own antiquity.

Mahmoud Mukhtar, *Nahdat Misr*, red granite statue, Cairo, 1928 – seen here in its present position near Cairo University, where it was moved in 1955.

Nahdat Misr was also the name given to another Pharaonist work of art, by the sculptor Mahmoud Mukhtar.[16] Mukhtar, who came from a village in the Delta, began art studies at the newly established School of Fine Arts in Cairo in 1908, then went on to study at the École des Beaux-Arts in Paris, where he lived for several years. While in Paris he made a marble statue called *Nahdat Misr*, which represented Egypt as a peasant woman lifting her face veil, standing next to a sphinx raising itself on its forelegs. After it won a gold medal at the Paris Salon of 1920, a nationalist newspaper raised money in Egypt to fund a larger-scale version. Mukhtar returned to Egypt after a nine-year absence to oversee the monumental work, which he decided to execute, with a team of assistants, in the distinctive pink or red granite of Aswan – a favourite stone of ancient sculptors, for whom it symbolized the rosy light of the rising sun. Although it took several years to complete the statue, and for politicians to agree where to place it, the iconography of the sphinx and the peasant woman proved memorable with its clean, modernist lines and for the way it evoked other modernizing aims of the age, such as the Egyptian feminist movement's call to abandon the white face veils that upper-class, urban women had donned in public under the khedives.[17]

If sphinxes, goddesses and peasants could all be counted on to evoke an 'authentic' Egyptian cultural identity in the 1920s, so too could Tutankhamun, as the tomb's treasures began to emerge into view. The clicking shutters of cameras, belonging to both tourists and the world's press, captured the spectacle outside the tomb. Guarded by Egyptian soldiers, Howard Carter and his team carried inlaid boxes, alabaster vases, chariots and other marvels to a more spacious tomb (the 'laboratory') nearby, which the antiquities service had given over for storage and work space. However, inside the tomb of Tutankhamun and at the 'laboratory' tomb where the objects were repaired, only official photographer Harry Burton took pictures of the excavation's work (see Chapter Six). Before his premature death in April 1923, the sponsor of the excavation, Lord Carnarvon, had signed a contract with the London *Times* giving the newspaper priority coverage and exclusive access to Burton's photographs.[18] Carnarvon hoped that proceeds from reselling the photographs would defray the mounting cost of the dig. It was a diplomatic misstep, to say the least: Egyptian newspapers were outraged that they were expected to rely on second-hand reports for news that was taking place in their own country. The *Times*'s British and American competitors were none too pleased, either.

There was also a widespread worry in Egypt that Carnarvon, his heirs and Howard Carter planned to claim the contents of the tomb for museums overseas, such as the Metropolitan Museum of Art in New York (whose staff, like Burton, were helping with the work), and for their own private collections. Carter had dealt in antiquities for years, and Carnarvon had a large collection of his own, formed with Carter's help. Rumours that some objects from the tomb had already been secreted out of the country were not groundless, and after Carter's death in 1939 Burton, as co-executor of his will, helped arrange the return to Egypt of several small objects found in Carter's possession, which Carter may have extricated from the Carnarvon collection after the Earl's death.[19] Of greater concern was the question of dividing the Tutankhamun finds with the Egyptian antiquities service, since this practice remained unchanged. Maspero's successor, Pierre Lacau, believed that more antiquities should stay in Egypt and that the Service should take a stronger lead in the division of finds with foreign archaeologists. In the case of Tutankhamun's tomb, the division should have been straightforward, since the excavation permit stated that the contents of intact tombs or tombs of special significance would remain the property of the antiquities service, hence of the Egyptian government. Dividing antiquities favourably with foreign archaeologists had become such an expected practice, though, that Carter persisted in staking a claim – and in sticking to the controversial *Times* agreement.

Egyptian novelists, poets and playwrights, as well as the popular press in Egypt, had no doubt where and to whom Tutankhamun belonged. The timing of the discovery meshed not only with the creation of a new state but with a formative period in Arabic literature, as writers experimented with prose fiction and abandoned classical poetic themes in favour of modern ones: like the Harlem Renaissance in America, Pharaonism was very much a Modernist movement, in literature as in the fine arts of Nagi and Mukhtar. The poet and playwright Ahmad Shawqi, who returned to Egypt in 1920 after years of exile in Spain, wrote a number of works inspired by Tutankhamun. Shawqi used the historic context of the boy-king's reign, which had restored the cult of Amun after its denigration under king Akhenaten, to draw parallels with Egypt emerging from British imperial tyranny. 'Pharaoh, the time of self-rule is in effect, and the dynasty of arrogant lords has passed,' ran part of the longest poem Shawqi wrote on this theme.[20] In the same poem Shawqi addressed worries over the fate of the tomb's objects head-on:

> Our forefathers, and their greatest [Tutankhamun], are an inheritance that we should be careful not to let pass into the hands of others.
> We refuse to allow our patrimony to be mistreated, or for thieves to steal it away.[21]

Of Turco-Circassian, Greek and Kurdish descent himself, and a one-time courtier of Khedive Abbas II, Shawqi might have seemed an unlikely nationalist, but in the face of the long British occupation,

Howard Carter and an Egyptian co-worker carrying part of a carved couch out of the tomb of Tutankhamun, early 1923.

nationalism was a unifying cause, at least for a time. The *Nahda*, or renaissance, of Egyptian culture went hand-in-hand with the country's own rebirth, and writers like Shawqi and the young novelist Naguib Mahfouz found a rich seam of images through Pharaonism that they could make speak to their contemporary hopes – even, or especially, where these hopes overlay inequities and anxieties among the broader populace.

Howard Carter, who had lived and worked in Egypt since he was a teenager, had miscalculated what the changed political land-scape meant for archaeologists, who for so long had been accustomed to dealing only with other Europeans for the administration of their work. Under Pierre Lacau, the antiquities service was still run by Europeans, and would be until 1952. But for the first time it answered to an elected Egyptian minister for public works. Infuriated by what he saw as government interference in the excavation, Carter downed tools after the second season of work at the tomb in February 1924, leaving the sarcophagus lid hoisted in mid-air over Tutankhamun's coffins. Lacau changed the lock on the tomb, which, after all, was government property. Only after a year of cooling-off on both sides – and a change of government in Egypt, effected under pressure from Britain when Egyptian activists assassinated the British governor of Sudan – did Carter return to finish the work. The *Times* of London no longer had exclusive access to news of the tomb; like other papers, they made do with regular bulletins issued (in Arabic, no less) by Egyptian officials. Carter continued to negotiate over the now-abandoned division of finds. In 1930 he secured a payment of almost £36,000 from the Egyptian government to the Carnarvon family, as compensation for the excavation expenses. Carter funded much of the rest of the work out of his own resources.

Transported to Cairo at the end of each season, the artefacts buried with Tutankhamun became the other star attraction of the Cairo museum, next to the royal mummies Ahmed Kamal had helped recover a generation earlier. The gold mask and coffins, the massive shrines and life-size guardian statues, and the hundreds of pieces of jewellery, clothing, sculpture, vases and furniture that made this minor pharaoh seem so significant, yet accessible, to a worldwide public, filled several galleries and attracted consistent crowds. As of this writing, they are being prepared for display in the Grand Egyptian Museum at Giza, whose development was interrupted by the 2011 revolution. Tutankhamun's own unwrapped mummy remained in his tomb, just as Carter and Carnarvon had promised it would, though its fragile, fragmented state (it has been interfered with several times, starting with the 1925 unwrapping) makes for a poignant finale to his once-trumpeted rebirth.

Circling the Square

Dreams of reawakening Egypt through its ancient past fuelled the Pharaonist cultural revival of the 1920s, but from the 1930s onwards, and in particular after the upheavals of the Second World War, nationalist symbols like Tutankhamun came to seem outdated, almost quaint. Tutankhamun fell from fashion in Egyptology as well, as if the glitzy finds and their political fallout were an embarrassment best moved on from swiftly. In the post-war era, and especially after the 1952 revolution, Pan-Arab unity and full decolonization came to matter more. During the presidency of Anwar Sadat in the 1970s, Egypt began to introduce free-market reforms aligning it more closely with Western economies, rather than the Soviet sphere of influence. Most controversially, Sadat signed the Camp David Accords recognizing Israel's right to statehood and earning Egypt the backing of the United States, notably in military aid. Under first Nasser and then Sadat, the treasures of Tutankhamun entered politics again, but this time as a diplomatic exchange to curry favours, rather than a colonial tug-of-war. Nasser's government agreed to lend fifty objects from the tomb to the British Museum in London in 1972, marking the fiftieth anniversary of the discovery. In the late 1970s Sadat agreed to let objects from the tomb tour again, this time to several American cities and later to the Soviet Union. It was the birth of the blockbuster exhibition, as queues for admission circled around city squares and street blocks: Tutankhamun has launched a mini-industry of TV programmes, exhibitions, books, museum merchandise and tourist trinkets ever since.

The recognizable gold-and-blue striped headdress of Tutankhamun's mummy mask, like the flat-topped crown of Nefertiti, helped turn both of these icons into useful symbols for revolutionary protest during the Tahrir Square uprising, and beyond. Like Nefertiti, Tutankhamun also turned up wearing a gas mask in Cairo's anti-government graffiti, and an Egyptian supporting the uprising at a demonstration in Paris donned a striped *nemes*-headdress for maximum visibility. Unlike the nationalism of the 1920s, or *al-Mumiya* in the 1960s and 1970s, these calls upon the ancient

Khaled Hafez, panel from the multimedia installation *Tomb Sonata in Three Military Movements*, 2010.

past seem as much outward-looking as inward-facing, drawing the West's attention to the problems facing modern Egypt, many of which are arguably of the West's continued making.[22]

A generation of Egyptians is once again stymied by the country's political situation, but when this generation turns to ancient Egypt as an expressive medium it does so with the intervening century in mind. For the Cairo Biennale in 2010, artist Khaled Hafez (b. 1963) debuted his multimedia work *Tomb Sonata in Three Military Movements (And Overture)*, which recreates the spaces of an ancient tomb. The *Sonata* combines music, painted canvases and light projections.[23] Scenes inspired by ancient art (sacred cows, goddesses, Anubis) merge with silhouettes of tanks, planes and snipers drawn from contemporary media coverage of conflict in the Middle East. The artist has said that the composition relies on viewers' visual memory of Egyptian art, with its distinctive arrangement of part-profile figures in ordered horizontal registers.

At first sight the military motifs blend in like so many hieroglyphs, but a second glance makes evident the juxtaposition of the ancient and the modern. This is not the timeless Egypt of Orientalist fantasy or nation-building myth. Unlike the modernist painters of the early twentieth century, who used ancient styles to depict idealized peasants, Hafez explores the explicit divisions and dichotomies of history, which are created in our own time through mass media and commodification as much as the ever-present triangle of military, political and industrial authority. As Hafez recreates it, the tomb brings ancient and modern, East and West, into a space and time that they share – but not without a struggle that echoes the struggles that have riven the Middle East in the past half-century. The tomb itself embodies the duality that Hafez's work relies on: it is both a place of death and a place where hopes of renewal are kept alive.

NINE

Still Looking

Death and renewal: with its massive stone ruins, time-capsule tombs and the mythology of Osiris and Isis, which turned the human drama of jealousy and revenge into a divine promise of redemption and rebirth, ancient Egypt has long seemed uniquely placed to speak to this theme. There is something suitably sombre in the way contemporary artists like Fred Wilson, Khaled Hafez or the South African artist William Kentridge deploy ancient Egyptian motifs in their work to address questions of identity and memory. Kentridge's *Carnets d'Égypte* series and his engagements with Mozart's Masonic opera *The Magic Flute* subvert the usual narrative of the European Enlightenment by drawing attention to its colonial roots.[1] Wilson and Kentridge have both explored racial tropes and ancient Egypt as well, Wilson in *Grey Area* and Kentridge in a video work that compares his own nose (Kentridge is Jewish) to the nose of a pharaonic image. All these artists are well versed in history, science and philosophy. In fact, Hafez cites the French philosopher Jean Baudrillard as one inspiration for his *Tomb Sonata*, with its critique of militarism set inside a simulated tomb. Baudrillard's best-known work addressed the simulacrum as a characteristic of consumer society, which he suggested had come to value the 'hyperreal' over the real. The simulacrum is not a replica of something that does exist or has existed. Instead, it is a copy of something that never existed but feels as though it should have, like Disneyland's pirate ships and all-American Main Streets.

In contrast to the serious mood of such contemporary art-works, popular culture seems to remember and replicate ancient

Egypt just for fun: adventure movie franchises, Halloween costumes, children's toys and bookshelves shaped like coffins, perhaps to hold your collection of Agatha Christie or Wilbur Smith novels. What would Baudrillard make of the Luxor Hotel and Casino in Las Vegas, which is based on the great pyramid and sphinx at Giza, with an obelisk thrown in for good measure? The Luxor complex may well prove Baudrillard's point, that the authentic, like the past itself, is well beyond our reach, replaced instead by the fantasy on which late capitalism thrives. When it opened in 1993 the hotel embraced an ancient Egyptian theme in all its public spaces, including a replica version of Tutankhamun's tomb in the casino and a Nile tour that snaked throughout the complex, past 'ancient' works of art. Although a 2007 renovation swept away these mock-Egyptian entertainments, the Luxor still amounts to a pyramid in the desert that replaces, and may even improve on, the real thing. For most of its visitors Las Vegas is more accessible than Giza, in more ways than one.

Even the most harmless-seeming fun marks a sign of the times, though. Throughout this book we have seen how different societies at different times and places have responded to what they knew or believed about ancient Egypt. Many Greek and Roman writers admired Egyptian religion and wisdom, although some satirized it as well, poking fun at sacred animals and images of animal-headed gods. In the Islamic world of the Middle Ages, some legends of buried treasure and secret chambers were as outlandish as an Indiana Jones movie, while medieval Christianity tried to map biblical stories onto the scarce travellers' accounts that reached western Europeans at the time. The Renaissance saw European scholars embark on fresh studies of ancient Egypt alongside ancient Greece and Rome, as all three 'lost civilizations' were rediscovered through a trade in ancient manuscripts and circulated through the new medium of print. The wisdom of Hermes Trismegistus, preserved in Greek, bridged ancient Egyptian and Christian philosophy, while ideas about the secrecy of his teachings shaped secular orders like the Freemasons and Rosicrucians, which brought elite men together outside the confines of the old aristocracy.

Replicas of the Great Sphinx, a row of ram-headed sphinxes, and two statues of pharoahs, outside the Luxor Hotel and Casino, Las Vegas.

In the social and political turmoil, and colonial expansionism, of the late eighteenth century, it was only a matter of time before some European state invaded Egypt; Napoleon did so in spectacular form. The cultural fad for Egypt-inspired decor that followed has often been called Egyptomania, but again this book has suggested that there was method to the madness for Egyptian-style furnishings and architecture. Imagining the Orient as an exotic land ripe for European pickings (and, for male travellers, pleasures) fit into the pattern of European domination that shaped the nineteenth century. A story like Gautier's fantasy of the princess's mummified foot is entertaining, but it is also an indication of which way power flowed between Europe and the Middle East, not to mention men and women. There were always alternatives to the white male imagination of ancient Egypt, too. Egyptian culture provided a rich seam of symbolism among African Americans, Afro-Caribbeans and in West Africa, while Egyptian academics, officials and artists have promoted their country's ancient past as a plank of modernization and national pride.

Much of what Egyptologists today cite as reliable scholarship on ancient Egypt goes back to the late nineteenth century, when the academic discipline of archaeology emerged in European, and later American, universities. The excavations that foreign institutions sponsored in Egypt, overseen by the Service des antiquités, filled museums in Cairo and overseas alike with Egyptian antiquities. This was also the era when routes to formal study and standards of academic publication began to separate self-consciously 'scientific' approaches from earlier efforts, which now seemed dilettantish in comparison. British, French, German, American and Italian scholars dominated the field, a picture largely unchanged today. Under the British 'veiled protectorate' (up to the First World War) and continued military occupation, the influence of British archaeologists and patrons was especially noticeable in Egypt, but no less controversial for that, as diplomatic clashes surrounding the excavation of Tutankhamun's tomb made clear. For Egyptians who wanted to learn more about their ancient history, knowledge of European languages was a must; a university-level programme for the subject was first introduced in Egypt in 1925. Only after the revolution of 1952 was an Egyptian archaeologist made head of the antiquities service, and only in the 1990s were foreign excavations required to submit reports of their work to the government in Arabic. Like other countries rich in archaeological sites and antiquities museums, Egypt has to deal with its ancient past in quite practical terms (administration, upkeep, security, tourism) as well as in symbolic terms that embrace the past for a sense of belonging and identity, or, in equally valid viewpoints, may treat it with indifference or reject it altogether. Not everyone wants a Tutankhamun T-shirt or a Nefertiti tattoo – or, for that matter, a revolution.

There is no definitive ancient Egypt, because the material remains that survive from the past are always interpreted through the concerns of the present day and filtered through layers of cultural memory. Ancient Egyptian art, language and religion all came to some kind of end almost two thousand years ago. In that sense, they were indeed lost – but they were never forgotten, being buried in our social psyche rather than the sand of an archaeological site. Excavating our own stratigraphy – how do we know what we think we know? why does someone care about *this* ancient Egypt at *that* point in time? – is as important as delving into the monuments and mythologies that any conventional survey of ancient Egypt can provide. That is what this book has tried to do. As an Egyptologist, I always encourage people to go to museums with ancient Egyptian collections, visit Egypt, read widely on the subject or watch films like *Raiders of the Lost Ark* and *al-Mumiya*, and television documentaries, if you like that kind of thing. But do so with a critical eye, and remember: wherever we look for the lost civilization of the Egyptians, we cannot help but find ourselves.

1 Looking for Ancient Egypt

1 Janine Burke, *The Gods of Freud: Sigmund Freud's Art Collection* (Sydney and New York, 2006), with the baboon at pp. 226, 232–3; Stephen Barker, ed., *Excavations and their Objects: Freud's Collection of Antiquity* (Albany, NY, 1996); Lynn Gamwell and Richard Wells, eds, *Sigmund Freud and Art: His Personal Collection of Antiquities* (Binghamton, NY, 1989). The website of the Freud Museum in London has information about his antiquities collection, with an online catalogue (www.freud.org.uk).

2 Paul Connerton, *How Societies Remember* (Chicago, IL, 1989); Maurice Halbwachs, *On Collective Memory*, ed. and trans. Lewis A. Coser (Chicago, IL, 1992).

3 For the Paris obelisk, see Todd Porterfield, *The Allure of Empire: Art in the Service of French Imperialism, 1798–1836* (Princeton, NJ, 1998), pp. 13–41.

4 James P. Allen, 'Language, Scripts and Literature', in *A Companion to Ancient Egypt*, ed. Alan B. Lloyd (Oxford and Malden, MA, 2010), II, pp. 661–2.

5 John H. Taylor, *Journey through the Afterlife: The Ancient Egyptian Book of the Dead* (London, 2010), cat. 161, pp. 306–9.

6 Salima Ikram, ed., *Divine Creatures: Animal Mummies in Ancient Egypt* (Cairo and New York, 2005).

7 Dieter Kessler and Abd el Halim Nur el-Din, 'Tuna el-Gebel: Millions of Ibises and Other Animals', ibid., pp. 120–63.

8 Martin Bommas, 'Isis, Osiris, and Sarapis', in *The Oxford Handbook of Roman Egypt*, ed. Christina Riggs (Oxford, 2012), pp. 419–35; Hugh Bowden, *Mystery Cults of the Ancient World* (Princeton, NJ, 2010), pp. 156–97.

9 Kevin van Bladel, *The Arabic Hermes: From Pagan Sage to Prophet of Science* (Oxford and New York, 2009), pp. 3–21; Garth Fowden, *The Egyptian Hermes: A Historical Approach to the Late Pagan Mind* (Princeton, NJ, 1993). See also Gary Lachman, *The Quest for Hermes Trismegistus: From Ancient Egypt to the Modern World* (Edinburgh,

2011), which is written from the viewpoint of a contemporary follower, but no less well researched and well written for that.

10 Brian A. Curran, *The Egyptian Renaissance: The Afterlife of Ancient Egypt in Early Modern Italy* (Chicago, IL, and London, 2007), p. 93.

11 Elliott Colla, *Conflicted Antiquities: Egyptology, Egyptomania, Egyptian Modernity* (Durham, NC, 2007), pp. 121–65; Israel Gershoni and James P. Jankowski, *Egypt, Islam, and the Arabs: The Search for Egyptian Nationhood, 1900–1930* (New York and Oxford, 1986), pp. 77–95.

12 David Gange, *Dialogues with the Dead: Egyptology in British Culture and Religion, 1822–1922* (Oxford, 2013), pp. 263–7.

13 Sigmund Freud, *Moses and Monotheism*, trans. Katherine Jones (London, 1939).

2 Forty Centuries

1 David O'Brien, *After the Revolution: Antoine-Jean Gros, Painting and Propaganda under Napoleon* (University Park, PA, 2004).

2 Ibid., pp. 92–4. For the Napoleonic campaign in Egypt, see Juan Cole, *Napoleon's Egypt: Invading the Middle East* (New York, 2007).

3 The account of Egypt is Book 2 of Herodotus, widely available in translation online (for example, http://perseus.mpiwg-berlin.mpg.de). For discussion, see Ian S. Moyer, *Egypt and the Limits of Hellenism* (Cambridge, 2011), pp. 42–83; Alan B. Lloyd, 'Egypt', in *Brill's Companion to Herodotus*, ed. Egbert Bakker, Irene de Jong and Hans van Wees (Leiden, 2002), pp. 415–36.

4 P.D.A. Harvey, ed., *The Hereford World Map: Medieval Maps and their Context* (London, 2006), with wide-ranging scholarly discussion. To explore the map online, visit www.themappamundi.co.uk, accessed 13 July 2016.

5 Okasha el-Daly, *Egyptology, The Missing Millennium: Ancient Egypt in Medieval Arabic Writings* (Walnut Creek, CA, 2005), pp. 48–9.

6 Edward Said, *Orientalism* (New York, 1978). For the impact of Said's work, and its relevance today, see Zachary Lockman, *Contending Visions of the Middle East: The History and Politics of Orientalism*, 2nd edn (Cambridge and New York, 2009).

7 Collections of the fragments attributed to Manetho, translated by W. G. Waddell, can be found in the public domain online, for example http://penelope.uchicago.edu/Thayer. For Manetho in the context of his time, see John D. Dillery, *Clio's Other Sons: Berossus and Manetho* (Ann Arbor, MI, 2015); and especially Moyer, *Egypt and the Limits of Hellenism*, pp. 84–141.

8 Lutz Popko, 'History-writing in Ancient Egypt', *UCLA Encyclopedia of Egyptology* (Los Angeles, CA, 2014); available at https://escholarship.org, accessed 12 July 2016.

9 Alice Stevenson, 'Predynastic Burials', *UCLA Encyclopedia of Egyptology* (Los Angeles, CA, 2009); David Wengrow, 'Predynastic Art', *UCLA*

Encyclopedia of Egyptology (Los Angeles, CA, 2009); both available at https://escholarship.org, accessed 12 July 2016; David Wengrow, *The Archaeology of Early Egypt: Social Transformations in North-east Africa, 10,000 to 2650 BC* (Cambridge, 2006); Béatrix Midant-Reynes, *The Prehistory of Egypt from the First Egyptians to the First Pharaohs* (Oxford and Malden, MA, 2000).

10 Rowena Gale and Renée Friedman, 'Buried in her Bark Pyjamas', *Nekhen News*, 13 (2001), pp. 15–16; available at www.hierakonpolis-online.org, accessed 12 July 2016.

11 Mark Lehner, *The Complete Pyramids* (London, 2008). For pyramids of early Dynasty 4, see Richard Bussmann, 'Pyramid Age: Huni to Radjedef', UCLA *Encyclopedia of Egyptology* (Los Angeles, CA, 2015); available at https://escholarship.org, accessed 12 July 2016.

12 John Baines and Christina Riggs, 'Archaism and Kingship: A Late Royal Statue and its Early Dynastic Model', *Journal of Egyptian Archaeology*, LXXXVII (2001), pp. 103–18.

13 Adela Oppenheim, Dorothea Arnold, Dieter Arnold and Kei Yamamoto, eds, *Ancient Egypt Transformed: The Middle Kingdom* (New York, 2015), pp. 319–22, which summarizes the pyramid sites of this period and provides further references.

14 Brian A. Curran, Anthony Grafton, Pamela O. Long and Benjamin Weiss, *Obelisk: A History* (Cambridge, MA, 2009).

15 Marjorie M. Fisher, Peter Lacovara, Salima Ikram and Sue D'Auria, eds, *Ancient Nubia: African Kingdoms on the Nile* (Cairo, 2012); Robert Morkot, *The Black Pharaohs: Egypt's Nubian Rulers* (London, 2000).

16 Jean-Marcel Humbert, 'The Egyptianizing Pyramid from the 18th to the 20th Century', in *Imhotep Today: Egyptianizing Architecture*, ed. Jean-Marcel Humbert and Clifford Price (London, 2003), pp. 25–39.

3 SACRED SIGNS

1 R. B. Parkinson, *The Rosetta Stone* (London, 2005), pp. 26–32.

2 For an overview of language and writing in ancient Egypt, see James P. Allen, 'Language, Scripts and Literature', in *A Companion to Ancient Egypt*, ed. Alan B. Lloyd (Oxford and Malden, MA, 2010), II, pp. 641–62, and his *Middle Egyptian: An Introduction to the Language and Culture of Hieroglyphs,* 3rd edn (Cambridge, 2014).

3 Peter Parsons, *The City of the Sharp-nosed Fish: Greek Lives in Roman Egypt* (London, 2007), p. 102.

4 Christina Riggs, *The Beautiful Burial in Roman Egypt: Art, Identity, and Funerary Religion* (Oxford, 2006).

5 Discussed in Jacco Dieleman, *Priests, Tongues, and Rites: The London–Leiden Magical Manuscripts and Translation in Egyptian Ritual (100–300 CE)* (Leiden and Boston, MA, 2005).

6 The best translation and commentary is Heinz-Josef Thissen, *Des Niloten Horapollon Hieroglyphenbuch* (Munich, 2001). A number of earlier

translations in English, available open-source online, give a sense of the work if used with caution; see also the overview of the text's modern history at www.studiolum.com, accessed 13 July 2016.

7 Okasha el-Daly, *Egyptology, The Missing Millennium: Ancient Egypt in Medieval Arabic Writings* (Walnut Creek, CA, 2005), pp. 65–71.

8 Daniel Stolzenberg, *Egyptian Oedipus: Athanasius Kircher and the Secrets of Antiquity* (Chicago, IL, and London, 2013).

9 Nicholas Temple, *Disclosing Horizons: Architecture, Perspective and Redemptive Space* (London and New York, 2006), pp. 166–73; Susan Sorek, *The Emperors' Needles: Egyptian Obelisks and Rome* (Liverpool, 2010), pp. 79–84; Brian A. Curran, Anthony Grafton, Pamela O. Long and Benjamin Weiss, *Obelisk: A History* (Cambridge, MA, 2009), pp. 165–72.

10 See Stolzenberg, *Egyptian Oedipus*, pp. 120–23, 200–206.

11 Ibid., pp. 76–7.

12 Parkinson, *The Rosetta Stone*, pp. 26–8.

13 Stephanie Moser, *Wondrous Curiosities: Ancient Egypt at the British Museum* (London and Chicago, IL, 2006), pp. 73–84.

14 R. S. Simpson's translation, reproduced in Parkinson, *The Rosetta Stone*, pp. 57–60.

4 Taken in the Flood

1 László Kákosy, 'The Nile, Euthenia, and the Nymphs', *Journal of Egyptian Archaeology*, LXVIII (1982), pp. 290–98.

2 Betsy Bryan and Arielle P. Kozloff, *Egypt's Dazzling Sun: Amenhotep III and his World* (Cleveland, OH, 1992), pp. 90–93, 138–9.

3 Strabo, *Geography* 17.46. There are several translations in the public domain, for example one by H. L. Jones, available at http://penelope. uchicago.edu. On Julia Balbilla, see Patricia Rosenmeyer, 'Greek Verse Inscriptions in Roman Egypt: Julia Balbilla's Sapphic Voice', *Classical Antiquity*, XXVII/2 (2008), pp. 334–58; T. C. Brennan, 'The Poets Julia Balbilla and Damo at the Colossus of Memnon', *Classical World*, XCI/4 (1998), pp. 215–34.

4 An accessible work on Antinous is Royston Lambert, *Beloved and God: The Story of Hadrian and Antinous* (London, 1984), but for more recent work on this complex topic, see Thorsten Opper, ed., *Hadrian: Empire and Conflict* (London, 2008); Penelope Curtis and Caroline Vout, *Antinous: The Face of the Antique* (Leeds, 2006).

5 Ian Rutherford, 'Travel and Pilgrimage in Roman Egypt', in *The Oxford Handbook of Roman Egypt*, ed. Christina Riggs (Oxford, 2012), pp. 701–16.

6 Molly Swetnam-Burland, 'Nilotica and the Image of Egypt', in *The Oxford Handbook of Roman Egypt*, ed. Christina Riggs (Oxford, 2012), pp. 684–97.

7 Casper Andersen, 'The Philae Controversy: Muscular Modernization and Paternalistic Preservation in Aswan and London', *History and Anthropology*, XXII/2 (2011), pp. 203–20.

8 Elliott Colla, *Conflicted Antiquities: Egyptology, Egyptomania, Egyptian Modernity* (Durham, NC, 2007), pp. 40–44.
9 Giovanni Belzoni, *Narrative of the Operations and Recent Discoveries in Egypt and Nubia* (London, 1820), pp. 212–14.

5 WALKING LIKE AN EGYPTIAN

1 Ernst Gombrich, *Art and Illusion: A Study in the Psychology of Perception* (London and New York, 1960); the cartoon appears on p. 2.
2 Paul Edmund Stanwick, *Portraits of the Ptolemies: Greek Kings as Egyptian Pharaohs* (Austin, TX, 2002), pp. 67–8 (Arsinoe II), 75–6 (Cleopatra III), 79–81 (Cleopatra VII). For the San Jose statue, which Stanwick identifies as probably Cleopatra III, see p. 118 (cat. D9).
3 Stephanie Moser, *Designing Antiquity: Owen Jones, Ancient Egypt, and the Crystal Palace* (New Haven, CT, and London, 2012), esp. pp. 81–119, also 121–39.
4 Chris Elliot, *Egypt in England* (London, 2012); James Stevens Curl, *The Egyptian Revival: Ancient Egypt as the Inspiration for Design Motifs in the West* (New York, 2005); Jean-Marcel Humbert, ed., *Egyptomania: Egypt in Western Art, 1730–1930* (Ottawa, 1994).
5 For two examples of Holman Hunt's Egyptian chairs in the Birmingham Museum and Art Gallery, visit www.bmagic.org.uk, accessed 14 July 2016.
6 Elliott Colla, *Conflicted Antiquities: Egyptology, Egyptomania, Egyptian Modernity* (Durham, NC, 2007), pp. 199–210.
7 See http://collections.vam.ac.uk, accessed 14 July 2016.
8 Robert J. C. Young, *Colonial Desire: Hybridity in Theory, Culture and Race* (London and New York, 1995), esp. pp. 118–41.
9 See Casper Andersen, 'The Philae Controversy: Muscular Modernization and Paternalistic Preservation in Aswan and London', *History and Anthropology*, XXII/2 (2011), pp. 203–20.
10 See http://whc.unesco.org.
11 Lynn Meskell, 'Negative Heritage and Past Mastering in Archaeology', *Anthropological Quarterly*, LXXV/3 (2002), pp. 557–74.
12 Plutarch's *Lives* of Caesar and of Antony both include discussions of Cleopatra; these are available in translation in the public domain, for example that by Bernadotte Perrin at http://penelope.uchicago.edu. For reliable discussions of Cleopatra in her own historical context, see Duane W. Roller, *Cleopatra: A Biography* (New York and Oxford, 2010); Michel Chauveau, *Cleopatra: Beyond the Myth* (Ithaca, NY, and London, 2002). For later representations – and misrepresentations – of Cleopatra, see Mary Hamer, *Signs of Cleopatra: History, Politics, Representation* (London, 1993).
13 Okasha el-Daly, *Egyptology, The Missing Millennium: Ancient Egypt in Medieval Arabic Writings* (Walnut Creek, CA, 2005), pp. 131–7.
14 Mary Hamer, 'Black *and* White? Viewing Cleopatra in 1862', in *The Victorians and Race*, ed. Shearer West (Aldershot, 1996), pp. 53–67.

6 VIPERS, VIXENS AND THE VENGEFUL DEAD

1 Edward Said, *Orientalism* (New York, 1978).
2 Judith S. McKenzie, *The Architecture of Alexandria and Egypt, c. 300 BC to AD 700* (New Haven, CT, and London, 2007), pp. 64–5 (sceptical that the tomb can be identified), 75; see also Robert S. Bianchi, 'Hunting Alexander's Tomb', *Archaeology* (May–June 1993); available at http://archive.archaeology.org, accessed 12 July 2016.
3 Herodotus, *Histories* 2.86–8.
4 Christina Riggs, *Unwrapping Ancient Egypt* (London, 2014), pp. 130–40.
5 Okasha el-Daly, *Egyptology, The Missing Millennium: Ancient Egypt in Medieval Arabic Writings* (Walnut Creek, CA, 2005), pp. 95–107, for Arabic sources; for the use of *mummia* in Europe, see Richard Sugg, *Mummies, Cannibals and Vampires: The History of Corpse Medicine from the Renaissance to the Victorians* (Abingdon and New York, 2011), pp. 67–77; Louise Noble, *Medicinal Cannibalism in Early Modern English Literature and Culture* (New York, 2011), pp. 17–34; and Philip Schwyzer, *Archaeologies of English Renaissance Literature* (Oxford, 2007), pp. 151–74.
6 Thomas Browne, *Religio Medici and Hydriotaphia, or Urne-burial Mumia*, ed. and intro. Stephen Greenblatt and Ramie Targott (New York, 2012), p. 136 (Chapter Five); available at http://penelope.uchicago.edu, accessed 15 July 2016.
7 Christian Hertzog, *Essay de Mumio-graphie* (Gotha, 1718). For a historical overview of the collection and study of Egyptian mummies, see Salima Ikram and Aidan Dodson, *The Mummy in Ancient Egypt: Equipping the Dead for Eternity* (London, 1998), pp. 61–101, and the more critical historical discussion in Riggs, *Unwrapping Ancient Egypt*, pp. 41–76.
8 Joscelyn Godwin, *Athanasius Kircher's Theatre of the World* (London, 2009), pp. 77–80.
9 Thomas Greenhill, *[Nekrokedeia]: Or, the Art of Embalming* (London, 1705). For a brief biography of Greenhill, see L.A.F. Davidson, 'Greenhill, Thomas (fl. 1698–1732)', *Oxford Dictionary of National Biography* (Oxford, 2004); available at www.oxforddnb.com.
10 Robert J. C. Young, *Colonial Desire: Hybridity in Theory, Culture and Race* (London and New York, 1995), pp. 118–41.
11 Debbie Challis, *The Archaeology of Race: The Eugenic Ideas of Francis Galton and Flinders Petrie* (London, 2013).
12 Grafton Elliot Smith, *The Royal Mummies* (Cairo, 1912), p. v.
13 Riggs, *Unwrapping Ancient Egypt*, pp. 67–76.
14 The story is widely available in anthologies and online in English translation, for example at www.gutenberg.org.
15 Nicholas Daly, 'That Obscure Object of Desire: Victorian Commodity Culture and Fictions of the Mummy', *NOVEL*, XXVIII/1 (1994), pp. 24–51; Ruth Hoberman, 'In Quest of a Museal Aura: Turn of the Century Narratives about Museum-displayed Objects', *Victorian Literature and*

Culture, XXXI/2 (2003), pp. 467–82; Roger Luckhurst, *The Mummy's Curse: The True History of a Dark Fantasy* (Oxford, 2012).

16 Bradley Deane, 'Mummy Fiction and the Occupation of Egypt: Imperial Striptease', *English Literature in Translation, 1880–1920*, LI/4 (2008), pp. 381–410.

17 For the full text of 'Smith and the Pharaohs', see www.gutenberg.org.

18 There are numerous accounts of the tomb's discovery, but fewer that take into full account the Egyptian political and cultural context. Exceptions include Elliott Colla, *Conflicted Antiquities: Egyptology, Egyptomania, Egyptian Modernity* (Durham, NC, 2007), pp. 172–226; James F. Goode, *Negotiating for the Past: Archaeology, Nationalism, and Diplomacy in the Middle East, 1919–1941* (Austin, TX, 2007), pp. 75–91; and Donald Malcolm Reid, *Contesting Antiquity in Egypt: Archaeologies, Museums and the Struggle for Identities from World War I to Nasser* (Cairo and New York, 2015), pp. 51–79.

19 Jo Marchant, *The Shadow King: The Bizarre Afterlife of King Tut's Mummy* (Boston, MA, 2013).

7 OUT OF AFRICA

1 Debbie Challis, *The Archaeology of Race: The Eugenic Ideas of Francis Galton and Flinders Petrie* (London, 2013), pp. 21–44.

2 Nicholas Grindle, 'Our Own Imperfect Knowledge: Petrus Camper and the Search for an "Ideal Form"', *RES*, 31 (1997), pp. 139–48; Miriam C. Meijer, *Race and Aesthetics in the Anthropology of Petrus Camper (1722–1789)* (Amsterdam, 1999).

3 Christina Riggs, 'An Autopsic Art: Drawings of "Dr Granville's Mummy" in the Royal Society Archives', *Royal Society Notes and Records*, LXX (2016), pp. 107–33.

4 Timothy Champion, 'Beyond Egyptology: Egypt in 19th and 20th Century Archaeology and Anthropology', in *The Wisdom of Egypt: Changing Visions through the Ages*, ed. Peter Ucko and Timothy Champion (London, 2003), pp. 161–85; Dana D. Nelson, *National Manhood: Capitalist Citizenship and the Imagined Fraternity of White Men* (Durham, NC, and London, 1998), pp. 102–34; Robert Bernasconi, 'Black Skin, White Skulls: The Nineteenth Century Debate over the Racial Identity of the Ancient Egyptians', *Parallax*, XIII/2 (2007), pp. 6–20.

5 See the editor's note prefacing a new scholarly edition of the book: Josiah Clark Nott and George Robins Gliddon, *Types of Mankind* [1854], ed. Robert Bernasconi (Bristol, 2002).

6 Challis, *Archaeology of Race*.

7 Jo Marchant, *The Shadow King: The Bizarre Afterlife of King Tut's Mummy* (Boston, MA, 2013), pp. 160–61, with press reports online, especially through the website of sponsor *National Geographic* (for example Brian Handwerk, 'King Tut's New Face: Behind the Forensic Reconstruction', 11 May 2005, http://news.nationalgeographic.com, accessed 16 July 2016.)

8 Scott Trafton, *Egypt Land: Race and Nineteenth-century American Egyptomania* (Durham, NC, 2004).

9 Ibid., pp. 63–84. See also Stephen Howe, *Afrocentrism: Mythical Pasts and Imagined Homes* (London and New York, 1998), pp. 35–58; Robin Derricourt, *Antiquity Imagined: The Remarkable Legacy of Egypt and the Ancient Near East* (London, 2015), pp. 130–57.

10 W.E.B. Du Bois, *The Souls of Black Folk* (Chicago, IL, 1903), p. 3.

11 Nathan Irvin Huggins, *Harlem Renaissance* (New York and Oxford, 1972, rev. 2007); Kevin Hillstrom, *Defining Moments: The Harlem Renaissance* (Chicago, IL, 2011).

12 Renée Ater, 'Making History: Meta Warrick Fuller's "Ethiopia"', *American Art*, XVII/3 (2003), pp. 12–31.

13 Sieglinde Lemke, *Primitivist Modernism: Black Culture and the Origins of Transatlantic Modernism* (Oxford, 1998), pp. 48–52. For more information on the artist see www.loismailoujones.com.

14 Cheikh Anta Diop, *The African Origin of Civilization: Myth or Reality* (New York, 1974), pp. 153–5, 179–201. On Diop, see Howe, *Afrocentrism*, pp. 163–92; Derricourt, *Antiquity Imagined*, pp. 157–9.

15 Howe, *Afrocentrism*, pp. 230–39; Derricourt, *Antiquity Imagined*, pp. 159–67.

16 Martin Bernal, *Black Athena: The Afroasiatic Roots of Classical Civilization*, vol. I: *The Fabrication of Ancient Greece, 1785–1985* (New Brunswick, NJ, 1987). There is an extensive literature, including Howe, *Afrocentrism*, pp. 193–211, and Derricourt, *Antiquity Imagined*, pp. 167–9. See also Jacques Berlinerblau, *Heresy in the University: The Black Athena Controversy and the Responsibilities of American Intellectuals* (New Brunswick, NJ, and London, 1999); Robert J. C. Young, 'The Afterlives of Black Athena', in *African Athena: New Agendas*, ed. Daniel Orrells et al. (Oxford, 2011), pp. 174–88.

17 Ferdinand de Jong and Michael Rowlands, 'Postconflict Heritage', *Journal of Material Culture*, XIII/2 (2008), pp. 131–4.

8 COUNTING THE YEARS

1 In addition to several websites devoted to revolutionary graffiti, see Soraya Morayef, 'Pharaonic Street Art: The Challenge of Translation', pp. 194–207, and John Johnston, 'Democratic Walls: Street Art as Public Pedagogy', pp. 178–93, in *Translating Dissent: Voices from and with the Egyptian Revolution*, ed. Mona Baker (London and New York, 2016).

2 Donald Malcolm Reid, *Whose Pharaohs? Archaeology, Museums, and Egyptian National Identity from Napoleon to World War I* (Berkeley, CA, 2002), pp. 50–54, 96–8, 108–12.

3 George R. Gliddon, *An Appeal to the Antiquaries of Europe on the Destruction of the Monuments of Egypt* (London, 1840); the work is often cited approvingly by Egyptologists.

4 Reid, *Whose Pharaohs?*, pp. 54–8.

5 Ibid., pp. 93–108.

6 Anne Clément, 'Rethinking "Peasant Consciousness" in Colonial Egypt: An Exploration of the Performance of Folksongs by Upper Egyptian Agricultural Workers on the Archaeological Excavation Sites of Karnak and Dendera at the Turn of the Twentieth Century (1885–1914)', *History and Anthropology*, XXI/2 (2010), pp. 73–100; Nathan J. Brown, 'Who Abolished Corvée Labour in Egypt and Why?', *Past and Present*, CXLIV/1 (1994), pp. 116–37.

7 Reid, *Whose Pharaohs?*, pp. 116–18 (on the School), 179–81, 230–34 (on Ali Mubarak). For Mubarak, see also Darrell Dykstra, 'Pyramids, Prophets, and Progress: Ancient Egypt in the Writings of Ali Mubarak', *Journal of the American Oriental Society*, CXIV/1 (1994), pp. 54–65.

8 Reid, *Whose Pharaohs?*, pp. 186–9, 201–4; Reid, *Contesting Antiquity in Egypt: Archaeologies, Museums and the Struggle for Identities from World War I to Nasser* (Cairo and New York, 2015), pp. 29–33.

9 Juan R. I. Cole, *Colonialism and Revolution in the Middle East: Social and Cultural Origins of Egypt's Urabi Movement* (Princeton, NJ, 1993).

10 Christina Riggs, *Unwrapping Ancient Egypt* (London, 2014), pp. 61–7.

11 Gaston Maspero, 'Rapport sur la trouvaille de Déir-el-Bahari', *Bulletin de l'Institut d'Égypte*, 2nd ser., 2 (1881), p. 135.

12 See Riggs, *Unwrapping Ancient Egypt*, pp. 192–4, 198–201.

13 Dalia Assam, 'Archaeologist Campaigns for Removal of Mummies from Egyptian Museum', *Asharq al-Awsat*, 4 February 2015, www.english.awsat. com, accessed 12 July 2016.

14 Elliott Colla, 'Shadi Abd Al-Salam's *Al-Mumiya*: Ambivalence and the Egyptian Nation-state', in *Beyond Colonialism and Nationalism in the Maghrib: History, Culture, and Politics*, ed. Ali Abdullatif Ahmida (New York, 2010), pp. 109–43.

15 Reid, *Contesting Antiquity*, pp. 44–5; Patrick Kane, *The Politics of Art in Modern Egypt: Aesthetics, Ideology and Nation-building* (London, 2013), pp. 24–32, 38–45; Caroline Williams, 'Twentieth-century Egyptian Art: The Pioneers, 1920–52', in *Re-Envisioning Egypt, 1919–1952*, ed. Arthur Goldschmidt et al. (Cairo and New York, 2005), pp. 431–2.

16 Reid, *Contesting Antiquity*, pp. 44–7, 128–30; Kane, *The Politics of Art*, pp. 28–31; Williams, 'Twentieth-century Egyptian Art', pp. 428–9; Alexandra Dika Seggerman, 'Mahmoud Mukhtar: "The First Sculptor from the Land of Sculpture"', *World Art*, IV/1 (2014), pp. 27–46.

17 On feminism's role in (and critique of) Egyptian nationalism, see Beth Baron, *Egypt as a Woman: Nationalism, Gender, and Politics* (Cairo, 2005).

18 Discussed in several accounts of the discovery, such as T.G.H. James, *Howard Carter: The Path to Tutankhamun* (London and New York, 1992, rev. 2001), pp. 277–81, 328–30, 480–85.

19 Ibid., pp. 447–8, 469–71.

20 Elliott Colla, *Conflicted Antiquities: Egyptology, Egyptomania, Egyptian Modernity* (Durham, NC, 2007), p. 220.

21 Ibid., p. 222.

22 On this subject see Timothy Mitchell, *Rule of Experts: Egypt, Techno-politics, Modernity* (Berkeley, CA, 2002).

23 Jessica Winegar, 'Khaled Hafez: The Art of Dichotomy', *Contemporary Practice*, II (2008), unpaginated. See the Cairo Biennale installation on the artist's website at www.khaledhafez.net, accessed 16 July 2016; the work also appeared in Hafez's recent solo exhibition 'A Temple for Extended Days', at the Ayyam Gallery, Dubai, see www.ayyamgallery.com, accessed 16 July 2016.

9 STILL LOOKING

1 William Kentridge, *Carnets d'Égypte* (Paris, 2010), and see the artist's gallery website, www.goodman-gallery.com, accessed 16 July 2016.

Allen, James P., 'Language, Scripts and Literature', in *A Companion to Ancient Egypt*, ed. Alan B. Lloyd (Oxford and Malden, MA, 2010), vol. II, pp. 641–62
—, *Middle Egyptian: An Introduction to the Language and Culture of Hieroglyphs*, 3rd edn (Cambridge, 2014)
Andersen, Casper, 'The Philae Controversy: Muscular Modernization and Paternalistic Preservation in Aswan and London', *History and Anthropology*, XXII/2 (2011), pp. 203–20
Assam, Dalia, 'Archaeologist Campaigns for Removal of Mummies from Egyptian Museum', *Asharq al-Awsat*, 4 February 2015, www.english.awsat.com, accessed 12 July 2016
Ater, Renée, 'Making History: Meta Warrick Fuller's "Ethiopia"', *American Art*, XVII/3 (2003), pp. 12–31
Baines, John, and Christina Riggs, 'Archaism and Kingship: A Late Royal Statue and its Early Dynastic Model', *Journal of Egyptian Archaeology*, LXXXVII (2001), pp. 103–18
Barker, Stephen, ed., *Excavations and their Objects: Freud's Collection of Antiquity* (Albany, NY, 1996)
Baron, Beth, *Egypt as a Woman: Nationalism, Gender, and Politics* (Cairo, 2005)
Beitak, Manfred, *Avaris, The Capital of the Hyksos: Recent Excavations at Tell el-Daba* (London, 1996)
Belzoni, Giovanni, *Narrative of the Operations and Recent Discoveries in Egypt and Nubia* (London, 1820)
Berlinerblau, Jacques, *Heresy in the University: The 'Black Athena' Controversy and the Responsibilities of American Intellectuals* (New Brunswick, NJ, and London, 1999)
Bernal, Martin, *Black Athena: The Afroasiatic Roots of Classical Civilization*, vol. I: *The Fabrication of Ancient Greece, 1785–1985* (New Brunswick, NJ, 1987)
Bernasconi, Robert, 'Black Skin, White Skulls: The Nineteenth Century Debate Over the Racial Identity of the Ancient Egyptians', *Parallax*, XIII/2 (2007), pp. 6–20

Bianchi, Robert S., 'Hunting Alexander's Tomb', *Archaeology* (May–June 1993);
available at http://archive.archaeology.org

van Bladel, Kevin, *The Arabic Hermes: From Pagan Sage to Prophet of Science*
(Oxford and New York, 2009)

Bommas, Martin, 'Isis, Osiris, and Sarapis', in *The Oxford Handbook of Roman
Egypt*, ed. Christina Riggs (Oxford, 2012), pp. 419–35

Bowden, Hugh, *Mystery Cults of the Ancient World* (Princeton, NJ, 2010)

Brennan, T. C., 'The Poets Julia Balbilla and Damo at the Colossus of Memnon',
Classical World, XCI/4 (1998), pp. 215–34

Brown, Nathan J., 'Who Abolished Corvée Labour in Egypt and Why?', *Past
and Present*, CXLIV/1 (1994), pp. 116–37

Bryan, Betsy, and Arielle P. Kozloff, *Egypt's Dazzling Sun: Amenhotep III and
his World* (Cleveland, OH, 1992)

Burke, Janine, *The Gods of Freud: Sigmund Freud's Art Collection* (Sydney and
New York, 2006)

Bussmann, Richard, 'Pyramid Age: Huni to Radjedef', UCLA *Encyclopedia of
Egyptology* (Los Angeles, CA, 2015); available at https://escholarship.org,
accessed 12 July 2016

Challis, Debbie, *The Archaeology of Race: The Eugenic Ideas of Francis Galton
and Flinders Petrie* (London, 2013)

Champion, Timothy, 'Beyond Egyptology: Egypt in 19th and 20th Century
Archaeology and Anthropology', in *The Wisdom of Egypt: Changing
Visions through the Ages*, ed. Peter Ucko and Timothy Champion
(London, 2003), pp. 161–85

Chauveau, Michel, *Cleopatra: Beyond the Myth* (Ithaca, NY, and London, 2002)

Clément, Anne, 'Rethinking "Peasant Consciousness" in Colonial Egypt:
An Exploration of the Performance of Folksongs by Upper Egyptian
Agricultural Workers on the Archaeological Excavation Sites of Karnak
and Dendera at the Turn of the Twentieth Century (1885–1914)', *History
and Anthropology*, XXII/2 (2010), pp. 73–100

Cole, Juan R. I., *Colonialism and Revolution in the Middle East: Social and
Cultural Origins of Egypt's Urabi Movement* (Princeton, NJ, 1993)

—, *Napoleon's Egypt: Invading the Middle East* (New York, 2007)

Colla, Elliott, *Conflicted Antiquities: Egyptology, Egyptomania, Egyptian
Modernity* (Durham, NC, 2007)

—, 'Shadi Abd Al-Salam's *Al-Mumiya*: Ambivalence and the Egyptian Nation-
state', in *Beyond Colonialism and Nationalism in the Maghrib: History,
Culture, and Politics*, ed. Ali Abdullatif Ahmida (New York, 2010), pp.
109–43

Connerton, Paul, *How Societies Remember* (Cambridge, 1989)

Curl, James Stevens, *The Egyptian Revival: Ancient Egypt as the Inspiration for
Design Motifs in the West* (New York, 2005)

Curran, Brian A., *The Egyptian Renaissance: The Afterlife of Ancient Egypt in
Early Modern Italy* (Chicago, IL, and London, 2007)

—, Anthony Grafton, Pamela O. Long and Benjamin Weiss, *Obelisk: A History*
(Cambridge, MA, 2009)

Curtis, Penelope, and Caroline Vout, *Antinous: The Face of the Antique* (Leeds, 2006)

Daly, Nicholas, 'That Obscure Object of Desire: Victorian Commodity Culture and Fictions of the Mummy', *NOVEL*, XXVIII/1 (1994), pp. 24–51

el-Daly, Okasha, *Egyptology, The Missing Millennium: Ancient Egypt in Medieval Arabic Writings* (Walnut Creek, CA, 2005)

Davidson, L.A.F., 'Greenhill, Thomas (fl. 1698–1732)', *Oxford Dictionary of National Biography* (Oxford, 2004); available at www.oxforddnb.com

de Jong, Ferdinand, and Michael Rowlands, 'Postconflict Heritage', *Journal of Material Culture*, XIII/2 (2008), pp. 131–4

Deane, Bradley, 'Mummy Fiction and the Occupation of Egypt: Imperial Striptease', *English Literature in Translation, 1880–1920*, LI/4 (2008), pp. 381–410

Derricourt, Robin, *Antiquity Imagined: The Remarkable Legacy of Egypt and the Ancient Near East* (London, 2015)

Dieleman, Jacco, *Priests, Tongues, and Rites: The London–Leiden Magical Manuscripts and Translation in Egyptian Ritual (100–300 CE)* (Leiden and Boston, MA, 2005)

Dillery, John D., *Clio's Other Sons: Berossus and Manetho* (Ann Arbor, MI, 2015)

Diop, Cheikh Anta, *The African Origin of Civilization: Myth or Reality* (New York, 1974)

Dykstra, Darrell, 'Pyramids, Prophets, and Progress: Ancient Egypt in the Writings of Ali Mubarak', *Journal of the American Oriental Society*, CXIV/1 (1994), pp. 54–65

Elliot, Chris, *Egypt in England* (London, 2012)

Fisher, Marjorie M., Peter Lacovara, Salima Ikram and Sue D'Auria, eds, *Ancient Nubia: African Kingdoms on the Nile* (Cairo, 2012)

Fowden, Garth, *The Egyptian Hermes: A Historical Approach to the Late Pagan Mind* (Princeton, NJ, 1993)

Gale, Rowena, and Renée Friedman, 'Buried in her Bark Pyjamas', *Nekhen News*, 13 (2001), pp. 15–16; available at www.hierakonpolis-online.org

Gamwell, Lynn, and Richard Wells, eds, *Sigmund Freud and Art: His Personal Collection of Antiquities* (Binghamton, NY, 1989)

Gange, David, *Dialogues with the Dead: Egyptology in British Culture and Religion, 1822–1922* (Oxford, 2013)

Gershoni, Israel, and James P. Jankowski, *Egypt, Islam, and the Arabs: The Search for Egyptian Nationhood, 1900–1930* (New York and Oxford, 1986)

Gliddon, George R., *An Appeal to the Antiquaries of Europe on the Destruction of the Monuments of Egypt* (London, 1840)

Godwin, Joscelyn, *Athanasius Kircher's Theatre of the World* (London, 2009)

Gombrich, Ernst, *Art and Illusion: A Study in the Psychology of Perception* (London and New York, 1960)

Goode, James F., *Negotiating for the Past: Archaeology, Nationalism, and Diplomacy in the Middle East, 1919–1941* (Austin, TX, 2007)

Greenhill, Thomas, *[Nekrokedeia]: Or, the Art of Embalming* (London, 1705)

Grindle, Nicholas, 'Our Own Imperfect Knowledge: Petrus Camper and the Search for an "Ideal Form"', *RES*, 31 (1997), pp. 139–48

Halbwachs, Maurice, *On Collective Memory*, ed. and trans. Lewis A. Coser (Chicago, IL, 1992)

Hamer, Mary, 'Black *and* White? Viewing Cleopatra in 1862', in *The Victorians and Race*, ed. Shearer West (Aldershot, 1996), pp. 53–67

—, *Signs of Cleopatra: History, Politics, Representation* (London, 1993)

Harvey, P.D.A., *The Hereford World Map: Medieval Maps and their Context* (London, 2006)

Hertzog, Christian, *Essay de Mumio-graphie* (Gotha, 1718)

Hillstrom, Kevin, *Defining Moments: The Harlem Renaissance* (Chicago, IL, 2011)

Hoberman, Ruth, 'In Quest of a Museal Aura: Turn of the Century Narratives about Museum-displayed Objects', *Victorian Literature and Culture*, XXXI/2 (2003), pp. 467–82

Howe, Stephen, *Afrocentrism: Mythical Pasts and Imagined Homes* (London and New York, 1998)

Huggins, Nathan Irvin, *Harlem Renaissance* (New York and Oxford, 1972, rev. 2007)

Humbert, Jean-Marcel, 'The Egyptianizing Pyramid from the 18th to the 20th Century', in *Imhotep Today: Egyptianizing Architecture*, ed. Jean-Marcel Humbert and Clifford Price (London, 2003), pp. 25–39

—, ed., *Egyptomania: Egypt in Western Art, 1730–1930* (Ottawa, 1994)

Ikram, Salima, ed., *Divine Creatures: Animal Mummies in Ancient Egypt* (Cairo and New York, 2005)

Ikram, Salima, and Aidan Dodson, *The Mummy in Ancient Egypt: Equipping the Dead for Eternity* (London, 1998)

James, T.G.H., *Howard Carter: The Path to Tutankhamun* (London and New York, 1992, rev. 2001)

Kákosy, László, 'The Nile, Euthenia, and the Nymphs', *Journal of Egyptian Archaeology*, LXVIII (1982), pp. 290–98

Kane, Patrick, *The Politics of Art in Modern Egypt: Aesthetics, Ideology and Nation-building* (London, 2013)

Kentridge, William, *Carnets d'Égypte* (Paris, 2010)

Kessler, Dieter, and Abd el Halim Nur el-Din, 'Tuna el-Gebel: Millions of Ibises and Other Animals', in *Divine Creatures: Animal Mummies in Ancient Egypt*, ed. Salima Ikram (Cairo and New York, 2005), pp. 120–63

Lachman, Gary, *The Quest for Hermes Trismegistus: From Ancient Egypt to the Modern World* (Edinburgh, 2011)

Lehner, Mark, *The Complete Pyramids* (London, 2008)

Lloyd, Alan B., 'Egypt', in *Brill's Companion to Herodotus*, ed. Egbert Bakker, Irene de Jong and Hans van Wees (Leiden, 2002), pp. 415–36

Lockman, Zachary, *Contending Visions of the Middle East: The History and Politics of Orientalism*, 2nd edn (Cambridge and New York, 2009)

Luckhurst, Roger, *The Mummy's Curse: The True History of a Dark Fantasy* (Oxford, 2012)

McKenzie, Judith S., *The Architecture of Alexandria and Egypt, c. 300 BC to AD 700* (New Haven, CT, and London, 2007)

Marchant, Jo, *The Shadow King: The Bizarre Afterlife of King Tut's Mummy* (Boston, MA, 2013)

Maspero, Gaston, 'Rapport sur la trouvaille de Déir-el-Bahari', *Bulletin de l'Institut d'Égypte*, 2nd ser., 2 (1881), pp. 129–69

Meijer, Miriam C., *Race and Aesthetics in the Anthropology of Petrus Camper (1722–1789)* (Amsterdam, 1999)

Meskell, Lynn, 'Negative Heritage and Past Mastering in Archaeology', *Anthropological Quarterly*, LXXV/3 (2002), pp. 557–74

Midant-Reynes, Béatrix, *The Prehistory of Egypt from the First Egyptians to the First Pharaohs* (Oxford and Malden, MA, 2000)

Mitchell, Timothy, *Rule of Experts: Egypt, Techno-politics, Modernity* (Berkeley, CA, 2002)

Morkot, Robert, *The Black Pharaohs: Egypt's Nubian Rulers* (London, 2000)

Moser, Stephanie, *Designing Antiquity: Owen Jones, Ancient Egypt, and the Crystal Palace* (New Haven, CT, and London, 2012)

—, *Wondrous Curiosities: Ancient Egypt at the British Museum* (London and Chicago, IL, 2006)

Moyer, Ian S., *Egypt and the Limits of Hellenism* (Cambridge, 2011)

Nelson, Dana D., *National Manhood: Capitalist Citizenship and the Imagined Fraternity of White Men* (Durham, NC, and London, 1998)

Noble, Louise, *Medicinal Cannibalism in Early Modern English Literature and Culture* (New York, 2011)

Nott, Josiah Clark, and George Robins Gliddon, *Types of Mankind* [1854], ed. Robert Bernasconi (Bristol, 2002)

O'Brien, David, *After the Revolution: Antoine-Jean Gros, Painting and Propaganda under Napoleon* (University Park, PA, 2004)

Oppenheim, Adela, Dorothea Arnold, Dieter Arnold and Kei Yamamoto, eds, *Ancient Egypt Transformed: The Middle Kingdom* (New York, 2015)

Opper, Thorsten, ed., *Hadrian: Politics and Empire* (London, 2008)

Parkinson, R. B., *Cracking Codes: The Rosetta Stone and Decipherment* (London, 1999)

—, *The Rosetta Stone* (London, 2005)

Parsons, Peter, *The City of the Sharp-nosed Fish: Greek Lives in Roman Egypt* (London, 2007)

Popko, Lutz, 'History-writing in Ancient Egypt', *UCLA Encyclopedia of Egyptology* (Los Angeles, CA, 2014); available at https://escholarship.org

Porterfield, Todd, *The Allure of Empire: Art in the Service of French Imperialism, 1798–1836* (Princeton, NJ, 1998)

Reid, Donald Malcolm, *Contesting Antiquity in Egypt: Archaeologies, Museums and the Struggle for Identities from World War I to Nasser* (Cairo and New York, 2015)

—, *Whose Pharaohs? Archaeology, Museums, and Egyptian National Identity from Napoleon to World War I* (Berkeley, CA, 2002)

Riggs, Christina, 'An Autopsic Art: Drawings of "Dr Granville's Mummy" in the Royal Society Archives', *Royal Society Notes and Records*, LXX (2016), pp. 107–33

—, *The Beautiful Burial in Roman Egypt: Art, Identity, and Funerary Religion* (Oxford, 2006)

—, *Unwrapping Ancient Egypt* (London, 2014)

Roller, Duane W., *Cleopatra: A Biography* (New York and Oxford, 2010)

Rosenmeyer, Patricia, 'Greek Verse Inscriptions in Roman Egypt: Julia Balbilla's Sapphic Voice', *Classical Antiquity*, XXVII/2 (2008), pp. 334–58

Rutherford, Ian, 'Travel and Pilgrimage in Roman Egypt', in *The Oxford Handbook of Roman Egypt*, ed. Christina Riggs (Oxford, 2012), pp. 701–16

Said, Edward, *Orientalism* (New York, 1978)

Schwyzer, Philip, *Archaeologies of English Renaissance Literature* (Oxford, 2007)

Seggerman, Alexandra Dika, 'Mahmoud Mukhtar: "The First Sculptor from the Land of Sculpture"', *World Art*, IV/1 (2014), pp. 27–46

Smith, Grafton Elliot, *The Royal Mummies* (Cairo, 1912)

Sorek, Susan, *The Emperors' Needles: Egyptian Obelisks and Rome* (Liverpool, 2010)

Stanwick, Paul Edmund, *Portraits of the Ptolemies: Greek Kings as Egyptian Pharaohs* (Austin, TX, 2002)

Stevenson, Alice, 'Predynastic Burials', UCLA *Encyclopedia of Egyptology* (Los Angeles, CA, 2009); available at https://escholarship.org

Stolzenberg, Daniel, *Egyptian Oedipus: Athanasius Kircher and the Secrets of Antiquity* (Chicago, IL, and London, 2013)

Sugg, Richard, *Mummies, Cannibals and Vampires: The History of Corpse Medicine from the Renaissance to the Victorians* (Abingdon and New York, 2011)

Swetnam-Burland, Molly, 'Nilotica and the Image of Egypt', in *The Oxford Handbook of Roman Egypt*, ed. Christina Riggs (Oxford, 2012), pp. 684–97

Taylor, John H., *Journey through the Afterlife: The Ancient Egyptian Book of the Dead* (London, 2010)

Temple, Nicholas, *Disclosing Horizons: Architecture, Perspective and Redemptive Space* (London and New York, 2006)

Thissen, Heinz-Josef, *Des Niloten Horapollon Hieroglyphenbuch* (Munich, 2001)

Wengrow, David, *The Archaeology of Early Egypt: Social Transformations in North-east Africa, 10,000 to 2650 BC* (Cambridge, 2006)

—, 'Predynastic Art', UCLA *Encyclopedia of Egyptology* (Los Angeles, CA, 2009); available at https://escholarship.org

Williams, Caroline, 'Twentieth-century Egyptian Art: The Pioneers, 1920–52', in *Re-Envisioning Egypt, 1919–1952*, ed. Arthur Goldschmidt et al. (Cairo and New York, 2005), pp. 426–47

Winegar, Jessica, 'Khaled Hafez: The Art of Dichotomy', *Contemporary Practices*, II (2008), unpaginated

Young, Robert J. C., 'The Afterlives of *Black Athena*', in *African Athena: New Agendas*, ed. Daniel Orrells et al. (Oxford, 2011), pp. 174–88
—, *Colonial Desire: Hybridity in Theory, Culture and Race* (London and New York, 1995)

ANCIENT EGYPT ON THE INTERNET

There are many websites dedicated to ancient Egypt and its afterlives – far too many to list here. For ancient Egyptian art and archaeology, major museums such as the British Museum, the Museum of Fine Arts, Boston, and the Metropolitan Museum of Art have wide-ranging coverage; many European museums such as the Louvre and the Museo Egizio in Turin have English-language content on their websites. Institutions like the American Research Center in Egypt, the Oriental Institute of the University of Chicago, the German Archaeological Institute in Cairo, and the Egypt Exploration Society also have active presences on the web and social media, with many digital resources.

The 'Artefacts of Excavation' website (http://egyptartefacts.griffith.ox.ac.uk) is a resource for tracing the division and distribution of objects from British excavations in late nineteenth- and early twentieth-century Egypt. The website 'American Egyptomania' is relevant to several topics considered in this book (http://chnm.gmu.edu), touching on aspects of Orientalism and Afrocentrism. English-language coverage of politics and culture in contemporary Egypt can be found on sites such as *Jadaliyya* (coverage of the entire Middle East, produced by the non-profit Arab Studies Institute), *Ahram Online* and *Egypt Independent*. The Ministry of Antiquities has a website and regularly updates its Facebook page.

ACKNOWLEDGEMENTS

As ever, I am indebted to Tom Hardwick not only for his invaluable advice on a draft of the manuscript, but also for many years of friendship, conversation and good cheer, over all matters Egypt-related. Master's-degree students in my 'Unwrapping Ancient Egypt' seminars at the University of East Anglia have contributed many ideas and inspiration relevant to this book; if only all teaching could include visits to the Freud Museum, followed by cake and coffee at the Louis Hungarian Patisserie in Hampstead. At Reaktion Books, I am grateful to Ben Hayes and Amy Salter for seeing the book through to completion with such helpful encouragement and patience.

■🖤🖤 PHOTO ACKNOWLEDGEMENTS

The author and publishers wish to express their thanks to the below sources of illustrative material and/or permission to reproduce it. Some locations of artworks are also given below.

© Alamy: p. 84; courtesy of the author: pp. 106, 121, 122, 146, 176; photo courtesy of Ayyam Gallery Dubai: p. 182; Library of Congress's Prints and Photographs division, Washington, DC: p. 85; © Los Angeles County Museum of Art: p. 114; © Metropolitan Museum of Art: p. 12; The Freud Museum: p. 15; The Griffith Institute, Oxford: p. 138; Harvard University Library: p. 131; iStock: pp. 16, 71; Trustees of the British Museum, London: pp. 20, 35, 75, 77; © Milwaukee Art Museum, Purchase, African American Art Acquisition Fund, matching funds from Suzanne and Richard Pieper, with additional support from Arthur and Dorothy Nelle Sanders (purchase M1993.191), photo John R. Glembin: p. 153; New York Public Library: pp. 56, 152; © Norwich Castle Museum and Art Gallery: p. 135; Rijksmuseum, Amsterdam: pp. 67, 91, 109; © Rosicrucian Egyptian Museum, San Jose, California: p. 100; Rupert Wace Ancient Art: p. 179; University of East Anglia Library, Special Collections: pp. 74, 173; The Walters Museum, Baltimore: p. 82; Victoria and Albert Museum, London: pp. 102, 105; © Fred Wilson, courtesy Pace Gallery: p. 160.

Hannah Pethen, the copyright holder of the image on pp. 42–3; Bjoertvedt, the copyright holder of the image on p. 39; Brooklyn Museum, the copyright holder of the images on pp. 47, 49; Miguel Hermosa Cuesta, the copyright holder of the image on pp. 186–7; Yann Forget, the copyright holder of the image on p. 88 have published these online under conditions imposed by a CCA Share Alike 3.0 Unported License.

Readers are free:

- to share – to copy, distribute and transmit these images alone
- to remix – to adapt these images alone

Under the following conditions:

attribution – readers must attribute any image in the manner specified by the author or licensor (but not in any way that suggests that these parties endorse them or their use of the work).